Embracing the Globe

M.J. OLDERSHAW

Dedication

To my friends, relations, acquaintances
who unwittingly helped me to write this book.

Published by
Robert Boyd Publications
260 Colwell Drive
Witney, Oxfordshire OX28 5LW

Copyright © M. J. Oldershaw

First published 2011

ISBN: 1 978 908738 02 8

Printed and bound by Information Press
Southfield Road, Eynsham, Oxford OX29 4JB

Contents

A Scot's Fling

Once upon a time, as the classic opening goes, there was a young lad of twelve years, living out his life within reach of the Highland heights. However, this was not the twenty-first but the end of the sixth century AD. The year was 597 which you may, if sufficiently knowledgeable, realize was the moment that Pope Gregory I sent St Augustine to England in order to revive the Christian church, which he duly did by sanctifying the future centre of the Church of England at Canterbury.

It was in the previous century that St Patrick, born in Scotland, had gone over from Wales to preach to the people of Ireland, and it was for three decades, from 563, that St Columba had crossed from the north of Ireland to the small, two-by-three mile island of Iona, skirting the west coast of Scotland, where he founded his ground-breaking influential monastery.

With this event, already his presence was felt on the mainland, and it would be another century before Lindisfarne, 'Land of the Winds' off the Northumbrian shoreline, became under Irish St Aidan a holy island. The inspired centre would produce beautiful, illustrated Celtic texts, like those on Iona, and then work towards its zenith as a Catholic religious body, finally attaining this in the second half of the seventh century during the lifetime of St Cuthbert. But this was for the future. The present was an interregnum gradually lightening any darkness.

Our youth, in the full flush of his boyhood, bore the name of Andrew, which was appropriate in view of the Saint's connection with the coast to the south of him where the Saint's body is, by tradition, said to have arrived by sea, resulting in the founding many centuries later of the University of St Andrew's in the county of Fife.

The saint's namesake, our boy Andrew, lived in the area of

Perthshire, but his family was somewhat original in that its members were lake-dwellers. His forebears had been living there for hundreds of years, receding into BC, Before Christ. It was an honourable form of life, going back to the time when humans came out of caves and built wooden platforms on stilts over lakes, or lochs, to protect themselves from wild animals, floods, forestation and other disadvantages. It was done in Switzerland, the Far East, and many places unimagined. Remnants of such timbers, below surface, have been identified in Scotland as late as the twentieth century. Some reached islands.

At the instant our eyes fall upon Andrew he is lying 'on deck' in the sunshine. It is the first really warm day of summer. The month is May. He is really fortunate in that he does not have to go to school, and is still young enough sometimes to be left by both parents to amuse himself. The loch is occasionally flooded, and in the past has received sea water, so there can be all manner of wildlife even underneath him! He has a piece of animal fat attached to a length of plaited grasses which he now lowers into the water, hoping a crab-like creature may take a firm grip, so that he can gently lever it up and place it in a bowl he has beside him. Thus he is learning direct from nature. Who knows what is down there – he might get a devil fish!

Mother calls. She has been dealing with domestic issues as most women do, but at the present time she is also in charge of their head of cattle which is grazing in the water meadow as usual. With the inviting weather one or two of the cows have wandered rather far along the lakeside and Andrew is being sent to retrieve them.

His father has gone up to Inverness, which is the central power of this region, in order to meet fellow farmers and discuss such mutual interests as organization and trade. He has some useful lowland areas where he can grow some arable crops, including corn and barley, the former very valuable for wholesome eating and the latter for healthy drinking. Wheat was introduced with the coming of the Romans.

It had been over three hundred years since the legions were recalled. Julius Ceasar had crossed to England in 55 and 54 BC but had retreated again. Then, in AD 43, Emperor Claudius invaded Britain for a more permanent stay. A modern attitude is that the Romans were already invited in by some southerners, leading to a protectorate with treaties. It took a while for the fresh troops to reach northern England but before the end of the century Agricola made forays into Scotland as far as Perthshire.

The year was 122 AD that the famous wall was started by the Emperor Hadrian, stretching nearly eighty miles across from Northumberland to beyond Carlisle, and being up to fifteen feet high. What is more, Hadrian came all the way to take in a view of the place it was to be built. Maybe he thought of it afterwards as part of the garden wall to his vast estate outside Rome! Many different nationalities were represented in those who erected, then guarded the barrier, and doubtless this diversity contributed to the variety of individuals who were still around after the withdrawal. This was in 410, which English speakers call the fifth century but the Italians the fourth, since they refer to the four hundred years.

Andrew, needless to say, was unaware of this last nicety. He was looking forward to the return of his father who had promised to take him fishing. The mighty Tay flowed not far away, and there was a delightful tributary of the river which crossed a nearby valley. Last August they had gone together early in the morning and were by the water's edge before the mist had risen. Andrew knew that this beguiling vapour could herald a particularly splendid day, and they had ended up wading out into the lapping ripples. There were no trout in the fresh water for them in those days, but they could catch pounders as well as tiddlers.

A very special treat was to trek to the coast. They knew a pathway which led right up high on a cliff face. Andrew could look down over a mile to the North Sea. The gulls and other seabirds always had masses to say. Since he had been a wee tot, like most children, he especially fancied the puffins with their superior bills of red, yellow and blue. Never mind that there were more on the west coast, closer to Iceland and with their favoured breeding grounds. The gannets also attracted his attention as they dived from their high perches right straight into the salt water for food.

Often he saw fleets of boats going off to fish for booty such as cod, herring and mackerel. As a real bonus he might see an old Roman barge-like structure with a rather terrifying animal or human head sculpted and painted on the prow with prominent eyes, formerly intended to scare those being assailed, but now just a curiosity for those plying trade.

Even more dramatic could be a Viking longboat, brilliantly coloured, with perhaps a dragon head and a row of bearded Scandinavians furrowing at speed through the wavelets with their oars. It was as though they intended to conquer the world which, in the next five centuries, they went some way towards doing, including in their sights the founding of Dublin in Ireland.

When not on these outings, Andrew had a pal in a neighbouring farmstead with whom to find amusement and exercise. The boy had a younger sister, a 'bonnie lass', and sometimes the three of them would go into the adjacent coppice to play. There were deciduous trees as well as evergreen, principally birch, elm, oak and ash. Not infrequently the children had dashed and ducked among the berried plants, coming out with daubed faces to form pictures rather similar to those made by their ancestors the Picts, whose name was probably not derived from 'pictures' as commonly supposed, but from the place-name Pecta. 'Scotland', in its turn, may have been taken from a local district, but Russia, even, has claimed its derivation from a word for 'port'.

When Andrew was not required by his parents to undertake some task, he was happy to wander on his own. He might run with the hares on the high ground or shadow some cross-billed finches among the pines, birds which would become almost unique to the Scottish area of the United Kingdom.

Alternatively, Andrew might enter on his own the local wood. He was never meant to go far, but one day he did find himself penetrating deeper when hearing some unusual bird call. Then it happened. He was standing close to a tree trunk when he realized, a few paces away, there was another creature looking back at him, similarly from behind a tree. The dark shining eyes were fixed upon him. What should he do?

Long ago, round about the sixth century BC when Greece was advancing towards the climax of its power in literature and art, Aesop, of whom not a great deal is known, wrote his most famous fable of all, giving good advice to children, namely not to cry 'Wolf' too often in case you were left when you really needed help. Now here was Andrew wanting assistance but too far away from humanity to receive any. He, like those after him, had heard of good, religious characters being able to stare down wild beasts, even tigers, which he had never seen, but somehow, not surprisingly, he did not know how to believe it and was not prepared to try it! He knew, too, instinctively that to turn and run would only encourage the chase.

He kept to the side of the track-way and employed the successful tactic of 'disappearing slowly'. The wolf, not in fact to be ranked with the most ferocious of animals, lost interest and moved away also. It all became just another youthful adventure. Wisdom has been admired in the ancients, who left their writings, but there is nothing to compare with personal sources for study, stories and scrapes!

Andrew lived, of course, before the initiation of printing presses and did not therefore have picture books to instruct him and help him to pass the time. There would be no illustration of imprisoned Robert the Bruce with a spider to console him. This hero, in any case, was for the thirteenth century onwards, and, on top of that, just a Norman anyway with a forebear who came over in the train of William the Conqueror in 1066. The Norse race, in one capacity or another, had been coming to Scotland and the islands even further north since prehistoric times.

After the land-mass connecting England to France sank beneath the sea current in about 6500 BC, making the twenty mile wide English Channel, all new-comers had, if they stayed, started as immigrants, and that is a lot of people! The Normans, in fact, were all over the place before William arrived, and were, in basic background, responsible for the first piece of literature to come down to us in the evolving English language, *Beowulf.*

The fair Anglo-Saxons with other races were, in addition, infiltrating continuously, eventually intermarrying. Before long, rather mysteriously, they consolidated communities with the resulting name from them of England. So during the formative years of Andrew there was not much cohesion or historical perspective. This did not mean united outlook had never been apparent.

Even when the whole country was much forested and no motorways existed, there was an unsuspected amount of contact from one end to the other, as the stone circles, almost unique to Britain, from the northern island of Lewis to the southern plains and levels of Wiltshire for Stonehenge and beyond, bear witness. Hadrian's Wall in AD may have divided the land, but after the Roman retreat the stony pieces which had been put up started to come down. The seventh century Saxon Church of Jarrow, for instance, in the county of Durham contains some of them, and it was there in the attached priory that 'the Venerable Bede' would soon be writing what is called the First History of England. One should not forget Gildas from the south who made an important contribution too. Nevertheless it was from Jarrow as well that the oldest Book of the Bible now existing in the world originally came.

Although the Wall, high or low, had long lost its significance, there continued to be skirmishes round the remains and further afield, to a large extent tit for tat. Meanwhile the Scottish went on developing their own mythology and collective memory. Waves of Celts frequently came in from Ireland, which helped preserve the Gaelic language in Scotland. Their racial descendants have always been perceived to show vivid imaginations and composition capabilities, but it was the dramatic scenery above all which activated the dynamics for wondrous sightings orally recounted.

Within the frame were gigantic monsters, not just Nessie of the Loch. Andrew could spot Orion the Hunter, with his three-star belt, in the night sky. The firmament could cheer him as winter approached with its long dark days. He was adept at comprehending the monthly cycle. He welcomed a bright new moon when its slender form appeared on the right and, after a fully rounded face, decreased to the left. The man in the moon beamed with full mystery and romance. Perhaps he could also see sometimes in the clearer atmosphere *aurora borealis*, the northern lights.

When the leaves turned vivid shades and before the deep snow, a party of men, avoiding any heavy rain, would rise to the level of the red deer, so arresting with their intricate horns when at their peak, and take a few for human sustenance during the hard freezes. Venison would be most prized for annual feasting. Logs of yule size were always plentiful, and communal merry-making sure to be supplied in equal measure to warm the heart.

Autumnal rains would be heavy, but with the snow storms would come the enchantment of the crystal panoply. The white outline of the rocky escarpments close to home would be familiar to the children. Moreover, Andrew would soon be rising to his manhood and looked forward to being taken to climb the Grampian Mountains further west. He knew some of the mounts, that is to say bens, and had been promised one day an assault on Ben Nevis, the highest summit in the British Isles which was all of 4,406 feet or 1,342 metres. Andrew would not mind which since the point would be mainly lost on him. Like those after him, he wanted to climb it 'because it was there'.

Mountains always have inspired and filled people with awe. Did not Moses, too, climb Mount Sinai twelve hundred or so years ago BC to feel close to the 'lux aeterna', in other words eternal light, and speak with God before writing down the Ten Commandments? There is purity in the upper atmosphere, as our quester has already discovered through ascending just as high as the munros.

In the present clear air below, though, any thoughts of wintry weather or indeed hard mountain climbing are far distant on the morning of which we have spoken. Andrew lowered the old protecting draw-bridge and is making his way down to the family ground beside the sky-reflected blue water, still as any pool. Most of the cattle are munching contentedly on their usual patch, but two of the browns have edged through the row of alders which normally act as a margin It is not difficult to shoo these back. The thought of frisky new heifers father may be bringing to join the herd can wait.

Now Andrew will be free for the rest of the morning lull. He can judge the time by the length of the shadows. Later in the summer season he might plan to cross the next brae and linger on the moors which would then be filled with the undulating sight and potent scent of pink deepening to purple heather. Above he might actually see the haloed head of a golden eagle, soaring and dipping over the glens.

Today he is satisfied to step up to the ridge in sight of his home. Nevertheless, through a single gap he can see the mauve tinge of distant hills and, a touch closer, the deep green of the conifers. Not far off are some fanning firs, with larches here and there to lighten the solemnity as the sun turns the transparent foliage yellower. It is an aspect which has not changed since primeval times. In the nearer clearing cushioned juniper sprouts. Having taken in the scene, Andrew rests his head back to get the full warmth of the mid-day sun. It could be the image of a relaxing boy in halcyon pose from a Dutch painting.

*   *   *

`Jamie, James, wake up!!' Why, it was his mother calling from downstairs. 'You had better come at once and have your breakfast or you will be late for school.' It was true, he had overslept.

What a dream he had experienced. It had covered many of his studies since the beginning of the academic year, and the present month was March. He could hear the wind blowing round his windows in their Leicester house and could see through a crack in his curtains some puffy clouds touched with rose. They were not broken up enough to be kipper, nor quite thick enough to be cumulus. He lay for a few more minutes to reflect on it, trying to remember what other names there were. His grandmother knew all the varied formations from illustrations on the back of a grapenut breakfast-food packet.

James did not mind school and had a lot of curiosity. He thought there was a fresh packet of cereal this morning, and he wondered what diversion there might be on the reverse side for him in this the latest century. Once out of bed he dressed quickly without more lateral thinking, so satisfying his mother.

He knew that in class shortly he would be learning about yet another holy connotation, for they were going to assess the life of Emperor Constantine, who might end up in Constantinople, now Istanbul, but who was another to get inspiration during his British stay, which was in the vicinity of York early in the fourth century. He is held to be responsible for the Roman Empire converting to Christianity. Then there were those, too, who went from England to the Continent expressly to spread the word.

This line of thought, coincidentally, covered mainly one early blossoming of British life, the religious. Music often helps recall the past, but fresh items can flit through the mind as well, like scanning along a bookcase or delving into an old ottoman. Each day does bring its own new learning curve and widening horizon.

Geoffrey Chaucer
1340 - 1400

Chaucer, England's first famous poet, was born in London on 25 October 1340. In 1359 while serving in the army for Edward III during the Hundred Years War, he was taken prisoner in France, and the King contributed towards the ransom to free him. It is not surprising he felt close to the royal family and he had a house which can still be seen today in Woodstock near the town entrance to Blenheim Palace, which land at the time contained instead the large Royal Hunting Lodge. During the year 1388 Chaucer took part in a Pilgrimage to Canterbury which resulted in his magnificent work *The Canterbury Tales.*

For this poetic creation he decided to use the English langu-age. This was done at a moment when it was still in a formative stage and in spite of the fact that in the medieval period French continued to be widely spoken in Kent. You do not need much knowledge of French to see how the author has sometimes intermingled it with English to create the desired effect. Occasionally it makes the rhyme for his heroic couplet.

In the Knight's Tale, one of the many life stories, 'nas' (Fr. *ne* and Eng. *was*), 'was not', is used in the couplet to pair with 'pas' from the French meaning 'pace, step'. In 'The Tale of the Wife of Bath' the French word *'richesse'* is used for 'riches'. Chaucer makes the point that there are better qualities than wealth to make both men and women worthy. He is certainly a religious man to some degree, demonstrably worldly wise, and these days viewed as commendably socially mobile.

In addition to French there are Early English words which can still be unrecognized, such as 'eek', 'also', now more commonly used in 'eke out', 'share, spread out'. Spelling at the time was markedly free and, when you come to read Chaucer, there will be a Glossary to help your understanding. One final example of an Old English word is 'begotten', which we still use biblically in 'Begotten Son'. We also continue with 'ill-begotten'. Americans frequently use 'gotten' in a past for 'get'. So one has interplay of root-form and tradition holding out to the modern day.

Chaucer married a relation of John of Gaunt's wife. He travelled on the Continent as far as Italy with periods too in Flanders and France – so you could say, with his cosmopolitan connections, he made a conscious and radical decision to write in English and promote the culture. At the same time he did display a certain amount of ribaldry, which could account for him becoming somewhat marginalized with the set-up under Henry IV. It is quite common to query his date of death. However, for clerical duties at the Palace of Westminster, he has a tomb and memorial in Westminster Abbey, which became the start of Poets' Corner.

Today we affirm the value of Chaucer in blending French and German derivations within the English context, giving a useful basis for the universal language English has become.

William Shakespeare
1564 —1616

Britain may have the world's primary literary figure but no one is now certain of his date of birth. However, we know he was christened in the parish church of Stratford-upon-Avon on 26 April 1564. It is surprising facts are not more complete about him though up-to-date research appears to have laid to rest the notion that he did not write the plays, for some people at least, while doubts still remain for others about the identity of the 'dark lady' of the Sonnets and inspiration for the poetry.

Shakespeare probably attended the local grammar-style school though this is not certain and, before becoming an actor and dramatist in London, married Anne Hathaway, whose cottage by Stratford can still be visited. Once settled in the capital, he performed at the Globe, Swan and similar playhouses, first under the patronage of the Earl of Southampton, then also to a degree Elizabeth I and James I. Incomplete records at periods of his life have to be accepted that far back.

Shakespeare returned to live principally in Stratford from 1611, staying until his death five years later, reportedly on St George's Day. His two daughters had grown up there in the country, the twin brother of the second having died early. No direct descendents have come down to the present day.

The poet's art seemed always vital to him. If Christopher Marlowe or anyone else had a hand in the writing, Shakespeare has been given credit. 'O Romeo, Romeo! wherefore art thou Romeo?' These romantic words naturally bring to mind Juliet on a balcony, but it is because the vocabulary is so apt that one retains the expression in the mind. In always seeking the correct verbiage for his plays, he greatly enriched our language. If you can acquire a selection of his prize passages, that will be a gem to keep. They have entered heritage.

For much of the twentieth century the two knights, Sir John Gielgud and Sir Laurence Olivier, competed in their appeal for the ultimate accolade. People vary in their favourite plays. Many consider the tragedy *Hamlet* his greatest. It contains the role in which rising stars like to prove their mettle. *Henry V* is popular, and always has been, among the history plays. Most of us might choose one of the comedies.

As You Like It embraces the memorable philosophizing of Jacques on the 'seven ages of man', somewhat modified these days. Very often one's introduction to Shakespeare is through *A Midsummer Night's Dream,* which is enchanting when performed outdoors such as at the Regent's Park Theatre where Titania's portrayal is paramount; and who can forget Bottom or the chink in the wall? The amateur production of the simple folk is fun to emulate with children. Perhaps the most enjoyed of the dramas by actors, both professional and amateur, is *Twelfth Night* which has some hilarious situations. There are also darker complexities to be fathomed.

Not long ago it was reported that a Russian lady had got interested in Shakespeare. In spite of English not being her native tongue she had penetrated his genius and was coming over to England to study him further. It would be a loss for you to miss out on this national and international treasure. One can build gradually on knowledge and information if one finds the bard initially difficult, as some do. The dramatist Ben Johnson, who was a friend of William Shakespeare and contributed a dedication to him in the First Folio of his plays which appeared in 1623, wrote the prophetic words 'he is for all time'.

George Frederick Handel
1685 –1759

The composer was born in Saxony on 23 February 1685. Similarly, J. S. Bach was born in the north of Germany with the same birth year, but their lives went in different directions. Handel travelled much and widely.

At the age of twenty-one he went to Italy to further his music studies, meeting musicians of the day, and thus he developed aspects of an Italian style which he retained for the rest of his life. On his return home he worked for the Elector of Hanover who would before long become George I of England, his mother being a granddaughter of James I.

Handel was at first primarily interested in Opera and, after the success of a composition in Britain, he moved across the Channel. When his former employer arrived, he must have felt even more settled. He wrote the *Water Music* for the King's progression up the Thames to his palace at Hampton Court in 1717. The royal party not surprisingly was delighted with it, and together with Handel's *Largo*, the item duly entered the light music repertoire where it remains as much loved today. Soon after his success Handel became a British citizen.

Then the following year, 1727, he produced the anthem 'Zadok the Priest' for George II's coronation with reflection back to the biblical crowning of Solomon. Handel did admirably fill the gap waiting for him on the local musical scene, one could say amply so, since he was a large congenial man who developed many friendships.

Fitting in with the English temperament, it is not to be wondered at that soon he found a welcome niche through the realm of Oratorio.

It is thought that Charles Jennen, who wrote the libretto, first suggested *The Messiah* to Handel. The words are based mainly on the Authorized Version of the Bible and the English Prayer Book.

The first performance of the work was in Dublin in 1742, followed soon afterwards with performances in England. The magnitude of its accomplishment has come to be felt worldwide. From the opening bars of 'Comfort Ye', through the majestic 'Hallelujah Chorus', one is drawn to the fulfilling conclusion. The French like to have it at Easter time, as Handel envisaged. British tradition tends to favour Christmas. It is for each to find his own consoling joy through this fine offering. Beethoven (1770-1827) himself gives reference with praise to the remarkable musical contribution Handel had been making from England. *Messiah* in its power of emotive response is a unique feat. Haydn (1732-1805) was moved and experienced this during an English stay, appreciating chorister finesse.

Handel lived the latter part of his life in Brook Street, a new development in central London at the time, and his house has been kept as a memorial to him. Brought up a Lutheran, he worshipped nearby at the Anglican church, St George's, Hanover Square. He wrote accompaniments to hymns, among them *Rejoice the Lord is King*, and interestingly had the arrangement of a tune adapted by the American Lowell Mason in 1830 for the Christmas carol *Joy to the World*. Its exuberance and optimism exquisitely capture the spirit of America, and the carol has now at last crossed the Atlantic to become popular on both sides.

Acquaintances said that G. F. Handel never completely lost his German accent. These days such a phonetic blend would just be deemed 'fascinating' In due course he was buried with full honours at Westminster Abbey.

Thomas Gainsborough
1727 – 1788

This artist was born during the spring of 1727 in Sudbury, Suffolk, the youngest of ten children. He loved his home ground all his life but his great skill as a portraitist took him away from his roots. In 1760 he moved to the thriving town of Bath where he mingled with the rich and famous, who came in the season to take the waters and to promenade.

Gainsborough showed such amazing talent in his craft and also had the reputation of finding with his oil paints the important likeness. He saw no ugliness, it would seem, but only the reverse in every fold and shadow. Individuals may not always appreciate his portrayal of wealthy decorative people in their apparel, though this was an age when at least a few members of English society were finding some ease and comfort in their lives.

Enter 'The Blue Boy'. It is a charming work, universally recognized, and once came to be placed among the six most famous paintings in the world. Gainsborough never went abroad which no doubt contributes to the essential Englishness of his style. Art lovers may feel that to try now to keep works of art within geographic borders is a bit like closing the stable door after the horse has bolted, the above-mentioned major picture in California, but with our increasingly international perspective, perhaps it is appropriate. Britain can go on creating appreciated novelty in a recognized national form as Gainsborough did.

The artist, with his family, moved to London in 1774, where he was a founding member of the Royal Academy. Before very long he returned in sentiment at least to his native Sudbury. He evolved his range, from society leaders such as the spectacular actress Mrs

Siddons, to men and women on the country estates of the landed gentry where he could show them, still in the admired finery, but with a rural background. This was a technique he personally delighted in developing.

Towards the end of the eighteenth century there was the young talent of Thomas Lawrence to join that of Gainsborough, Sir Joshua Reynolds and others. His picture of 'Pinkie' in her bonnet confirmed the local dominance in this field of captured youth at the time. The velvet suits, too, probably encouraged Frances Hodgson Burnett, before the end of the nineteenth century, to create the oft-quoted Little Lord Fauntleroy in one of her novels.

John Constable, who was another painter to come from Suffolk, soon continued Gainsborough's glorification of the countryside. But it will remain for his rendition of the beautiful people in his period that Gainsborough will chiefly be remembered. His house in the centre of rural Sudbury is now a museum and can be easily found there.

William Blake
1757 - 1827

England's poet, printer, prophet was born on 28 November 1757 in Soho, London. He stopped his schooling at the age of ten so that he could further his initial interest in art. He joined an engraver who provided him with the basis, not only for his professional work for other poets, but also for his own abiding life interests. He developed new ways of using his skills, and at the same time continued his own extensive reading. Then he began to write verse which from the start showed his own imaginative strain of composition.

He opened his own workshop where he was followed by his wife and younger brother, Robert. Unfortunately his brother died young and, since the two were very close, his loss left a marked impression on William. He claimed he could make spiritual contact with Robert and this deepened his other-worldliness. It is not therefore incomprehensible, in view of his unusual background, that the mystical quality is always to be observed in his craft. He wanted his poems to be accompanied by illustration and, using his own methods, *Songs of Innocence* appeared in 1789.

He was greatly affected by the hardships he observed in London and used this material for his *Songs of Experience*, which was added in 1794. Here is to be found perhaps his most famous romantic vision which begins:

> Tiger, tiger, burning bright
> In the forests of the night
> What immortal hand or eye
> Could frame thy fearful symmetry?

His favoured method of production was to create etched copper-plates and then colour each print with pen or paintbrush. That is how he wanted his poems to be seen, so there was no mass-production in his lifetime.

His first workplace was near his childhood home, but he did later move south across the river to Lambeth. Various other collections appeared in his name, and it was from the preface of one called *Milton* that the hymn 'Jerusalem' was taken: And did those feet.... 'Jerusalum' has become a great source of inspiration for citizens of his country. The piece was taken by the poet Robert Bridges and offered to the composer Hubert Parry requesting that he might set it to music. It was a marvellous and fortuitous partnership, first performance taking place in 1916 and then in 1920 to great acclaim.

So William Blake had to wait for more modern times to have his talents properly appreciated. There are now advanced methods of reproduction to provide something closer akin to what Blake desired for his engraved and colour-printed drawings. Probably the most stylish volumes to be published were those leather-bound for the Blake Society by the Trianon Press in Paris during the twentieth century.

Much appreciated now are his Job watercolours, under-taken for Thomas Butts in 1805. These reveal his keen biblical theology, which stretched from Genesis to Revelations.

Blake longed to see all people able to be free. This yearning contributed to his great originality and many faceted progression. He spent much of his later years down on the Sussex coast.

John Keats
1795 – 1821

Some English people respond particularly to Thomas Gray (1716-71) and his 'Elergy written in a country churchyard', others to William Wordsworth (1770-1850) and his poem 'Upon Westminster Bridge', but you will still find a great many people who, when touching on the subject of poets, will mention at once John Keats. He did not study at Oxford or Cambridge, like many major literary figures of former times, and some critics may consider his canon less worthy than others, but Keats used his language finely and hauntingly in a way modern generations have liked to retain.

The poet was born in London on 31 October 1795. He was trained as a surgeon but abandoned thoughts of that profession through his love of literature. He became a friend of Shelley, visited the secluded groves of Magdalen College, Oxford, source of inspiration for many poets, and like many of them too, made a trip to Fingel's Cave in the Hebrides of Scotland. You may know Mendelssohn's composition on the latter theme after his Hebridean journey.

Americans are quite often attracted to Keats, who did write in one of his sonnets, 'On first looking into Chapman's Homer', with great prescience of our unifying world, about the enthralling vision as Cortez first stared at the vast Pacific with a wild surmise. But wait a minute: was it not Balboa given the credit of being the first European to gaze at the Pacific, musing with his men? Never mind if it should be a bit of poetic licence. In fact the last named trekked there, not with first view by sea as many others.

The Odes of Keats are usually fancied among most readers as much as any of his other poems. When September arrives, it is common to bring to mind with admiration for his accurate perception the opening line of `To Autumn': 'Season of mists and mellow fruitfulness', though now with global warming they may be less marked and arrive later. Another evocative piece might come from 'Ode to a Nightingale', and there are familiar stanzas from numerous others. 'Ode on a Grecian Urn' reveals his respect for the art of ancient Greece.

The poet's love of beauty extended to where he lived. You can see a smart front door, once his, in a terraced row of houses near Hampstead Heath, and also his final home in Hampstead, London, which has now become a museum. You might have thought he was ideally placed for a good life, with the heath for physical exercise, visual inspiration, and healthy living.

Unfortunately, at an early age Keats became unwell, developing what some of the old records refer to as consumption, in other words tuberculosis of the lungs. He had his close friend Fanny Brawne (1802-65) and her mother to care for him. In 1820 he sailed for Italy and took up residence in Rome by the Spanish Steps, a striking habitation and a building which can also be entered today. The following year after his arrival he died and was buried in the Protestant cemetery there. The future of his final residence has become less certain.

As John Keats wrote in his oft-repeated line from *Endymion*, his second offering of three volumes, 'A thing of beauty is a joy for ever'. Where the English flow is spoken and understood, his verse will always be respected and kept for its appealing directness and natural elegance. A new age, however, would soon dawn when Victorians would love their omnipresent Alfred Lord Tennyson (1809-92) and might sing by the piano with appreciation, 'Come into the garden, Maud'!

Edward Elgar
1857 –1934

The composer was born near Worcester on 2 June 1857. His father was an organist and ran a shop for related wares which included the selling of sheet music, so the back-ground of the youth was very much with music but not with a great deal of professional training. He married in 1889 and his wife appears to have been of much assistance to him for he stopped composing in a major way after she died.

Elgar was aged forty-two when his *Enigma Variations* appeared. It was an amazing and unusual creation, the former because it was so successful and the latter because it was based on individual portraits of a number of his friends, though inevitably revealing above all himself. Its integrity was at once recognized on the Continent. The reaction was as though Britain's musical reputation was redeemed by this one man. However, many of his further works were considered essentially English and he did not immediately receive a big reputation abroad.

He loved his area of England, which was dominated by the Malvern Hills, and enjoyed participating in his Three Choirs Festival which takes place still today rotationally in the Cathedral towns of Worcester, Gloucester and Hereford. His presence continues to be felt in his locality, especially around his former cottage dwellings.

He was actually brought up in the Roman Catholic faith which is reflected in some of his compositions, such as *The Apostles* and *The Dream of Gerontius*, which accompanies the poetic monologue of John Henry Newman. Among his other successful achievements at home were his violin and cello concertos. Another piece frequently played, thus becoming well known, is his *Cockaigne* concert overture, inspired by busy London. All these works witness his innate dignity and abounding tunefulness.

Above all he demonstrated his patriotic pride through his group of military marches *Pomp and Circumstance*. It is from the first of these that *Land of Hope and Glory* has been taken and words at the time of Edward VII's coronation were added by A C Benson, the father of the humerous novelist who invented his characters Mapp and Lucia, since familiar through adaptation for the media.

It is not surprising that the composer was early knighted for his outstanding talents, and his reputation has continued to grow, particularly with the global syndication of 'the last night at the Proms', which is now performed annually live with a limited degree of changes. Together with *Jerusalem, Land of Hope and Glory* provides a chance by television or such like for the world to join in with some communal singing and sportive interplay. Word got around recently that *Land of Hope and Glory* had been used at a Mexican national event. It is good in this age of mass communication to know that original endeavours of all kinds can be welcomed beyond U.K. shores.

There has been a rich seam of music from Britain which has covered many aspects of different genres. It is now thought that the tune for the Scottish *Auld Lang Syne* was probably written by an organist at Durham Cathedral, the music for the U.S. national anthem, *The Star Spangled Banner,* by an organist at Gloucester Cathedral, and that the Australian *Waltzing Matilda* took its lilting bars from what was conceived long ago as an English military song. So one can say music from this island source has always been varied, and the traffic two-way. Nevertheless Sir Edward Elgar does stand supreme in most assessments of English serious classical music and his output now travels well.

African Hop

To take a trip to a wild-life park in the southern hemisphere or thereabouts has developed a cachet exceeding all others in the holiday stakes, for many at least. There is the combination of being able to live a little rough and close to nature, topped with the thrill of seeing those zoo animals, known since babyhood in all their various guises except the physically accurate reality, suddenly as near as we are able to get to them in the contemporary world.

From the welter of experiences of eye which may be received, none is more intense (or difficult to overlook!) than the elephant. After all, he is our largest land mammal. Yet his, or her, distant origin as a species was not on the African continent. Scientists tell us that, together with his now extinct early cousin the mammoth, his roots go back to the North American continent. Rather surprisingly it is the same with the camel and the rhinoceros. Even the horse, which the Spaniards brought back when they arrived in the Americas, from the sixteenth century onwards, were only bringing it home to its native land. Then too, the fox, we are told, eventually to become with hunting a traditional part of the English landscape, recorded through framed pictures, started in what has become the U.S.A.

All this is only a tiny fraction of the seemingly almost miraculous history we are given of the past, particularly through television with the reconstructed dinosaurs of the Mesozoic era, about 248 to 65 million years ago. More tangibly, when some local road near where you live is dug up, you may have been told of an incredible collection of primordial bones being surfaced. Perhaps the whole matter may have come to life for you by seeing one simple artefact or item like the remains of the sabre-tooth tiger, retrieved near Torquay in Devon.

That is another way of saying all these animals spread all over the place according to climate and conditions. There was quite an exodus from the North American continent, over a million years ago, by the Bering Straits land-bridge, which was again usable after the last great ice age that came to an end about 15,000 years ago. Thus was formed again firm land between Russia and America before the rising waters completely flooded it.

Among the animals getting across was the camel who ended up in the torrid zones like Arabia. Through the generations they produced a most useful hump for food storage in desert locations. Elephants also favoured the warmer regions and a small species has maintained its grip on an island of Indonesia. A similar example of singular unequalled survival on an island is the lemur, with its myriad family forms, on Africa's off-shore island of Madagascar.

By contrast, remote in China's rich, green inland preserves, have survived undisturbed large numbers of elephants. Herds did once roam, for sure, across southern Europe, and it has been suggested that an elephant skull coming to light years later on a Greek island, gave rise to the myth of the one-eyed giant race of Cyclops encountered by Odysseus in Homer's *Odyssey*. Such a proposition can, no doubt, if conceivable help to account for legends about which it is impossible to fully comprehend the source.

The Indian elephant became a creature of much affection, both for those in Asia and also for the British in their eastern encounters. Becoming, in fact, often quite domesticated, they have helped over the years in jungle tree-clearance by the removal of extremely heavy logs with the assistance of their trunks. Individuals have, as well, lent grandeur, yea magnificence, to stately processions and courtly celebrations. Possibly you have ridden on one in a zoological garden, looking down uneasily or confidently on other mere mortals? The capacious saddle is called a howdah.

Latterly the African elephant, with all the popular vacation offers available for tourists, has moved centre stage. These are to be unmistakably glimpsed in a remarkable number of haunts, and are still basically categorized as wild, though bands have been trained by the Romans and others. In South Africa there is the veldt or veld, name in lingo of the Dutch Boers for the wide open grasslands. There are elephants here and additionally in the more lush Botswana area. Even to the west, in the dusty desert of Namibia, far from the welcome waters of the Zambezi, there are herds able to live without assistance.

Further north, in West Africa below susceptible Mali, they have novelly been spotted in thickly forested densities of depths which might seem like nowhere. It is believed that at one epoch the terrain was more uncluttered for them, so long have they been naturally in their habitat. It is like the survival of a few crocodiles found south of the Nile delta where the ground has lost its moisture and been left wooded, in other words no longer seen as viable for them. Maybe these are distant cousins of St George's dragon from which he rescued a damsel in distress, creating the myth of England's patron saint.

The countries where most of the wild life of Africa existed at the dawn of year 2000, and where hopefully with thoughtfulness it may continue to persist and flourish for many years to come, are the eastern states of Kenya and Tanzania. It is here, in a fancied East African game reserve, that our attention is now taken and we get down to details. No, so-called useless, white elephants of course.

*   *   *

There is a herd of about a dozen adult elephants with some almost fully grown bulls, reaching the stage to join the other males who roam in a free but somewhat solitary way about the varied expanse of park land. The group which stays close together is made up principally of the females, and there are also a few young calves. The smallest of the young is called Ray, who is only a few months old and can still fit under his mother's belly. Gestation in the womb took nearly two years, and the period while he continues to suck milk, lasts for about thirty months with suitable vegetation on the side.

Ray's name may have come from one of his researchers, who are never far away and accepted as part of the scene. Nevertheless, it is a name to gladden his mother's heart since he is her little ray of sunshine. He has a cousin who is several months older and bears the name of Will. This, too, is satisfactory because he definitely has a will of his own and is able to teach his younger cousin many things, including a trick or two.

Their section of the compound, skirted by a river, is filling up with creatures. The heavy rainy season, which coincides very much as an English winter would, is over and the hordes of beasts who migrate across the current for drier pastures, which can be hazardous if there are crocodiles around, are back. This area of the park is actually very moist by March, with flood plains still covered with pooled extensions. That situation suits the hippopotamuses (or hippopotami), of which there are countless numbers, since they love to duck under the water, and the rims of their bodies, with a rosy tinge, can be seen all over the complex in its irregularities.

The elephant is the biggest and most powerful land mammal as we are aware. The African is even larger than the Indian and has bigger ears for his build. Ray could be called Big Ears and this he would not mind. He comes from a sizeable tribe, with an uncle said to weigh ten tons. Perhaps this is a folksy exaggeration and a bit over the top since nine tons, leaving aside tonnes, which make a little less, is considered already a Guinness-record proportion. One day Ray might acquire a third name, Jumbo, but this would be far away in the future, and not to be confused with the original Dumbo from an American film, another infant sugar sweet. Animals have been classed together `dumb', lacking our own speech facility. Ray cannot be thought dumb as the word is normally understood. He is all there.

The head of his party at the moment, the matriarch, is his grand-mother, the oldest among them and therefore the one with the most experience and longest memory, being over fifty in age. She can always be relied on to lead them to the best place to be. Her loss, when it comes, will be greatly grieved since elephants are emotional and need to observe a mourning period whatever the age of those who leave them.

In the coming morning, not particularly early, because they have been about to some extent in the night, the troop ambles down to the nearest waterhole. The other animals make way at their arrival. Size counts everywhere in the universe on occasion. There may be a heron or two who drink on, as they are comparatively slight, not taking up much room, and inhabit the world of flight, another conception. Up above, in blossoming trees, there are likely to be some vultures, not altogether concealed, their dark feathers preened, but these birds are not necessarily harmful. They just have to find methods to survive like everybody else.

Ray and Will go into the water for a wallow side by side. Ray is getting more adept with his trunk each day. Will squirts some of the vital liquid in his direction with this unique Dumbo appendage. All elephants like to roll in the moisturized earth, giving their wrinkled skin a good mud bath. They will likely be back again in the evening, but soon the prestige party is setting off across the flat savannah with a view to filling once more their vast bodies with sufficient nourishment.

Elephants are herbivores. They eat roots, grass, leaves, twigs, bark, fruit and nuts mainly. So you name it, they probably eat it. They have a great fancy for the acacia and its podded delicacy. If they live in a dry area, they can easily have competition from the giraffe who also likes it. To speak directly and to the point, the two species are rivals when together in some neck of the woods. What is more, a giraffe can be well camouflaged with its flecked coat toned to the sun-touched foliage. Never mind, the elephant has the final trump trick to out-manoeuvre the high necked, long tongued giraffe without further resort to the trunk. They can pick their moment to set to, barge their bulk and knock the tree down, reaching thus all top-most branches. Game, slam and match!

A shorter probable neighbour in this wilderness is the rhinoceros, who is ready for a hot sunbath. He has grown a thick skin against the world, appearing quite armour-plated in his long journey from the far reaches of our time capsule, well beyond the Stone Age. He can be extraordinarily benign, but do not let him mistake you in any way, for he cannot see too clearly and might charge. Remember that horn which may be in duplicate. There are two types of rhino. The so-called black and the so-called white. The latter is actually a misnomer from the Germanic word 'weft', meaning wide. He is physically bigger than the former, and both are in shades of grey, being darker and lighter.

Nearby you might equally spot a wildebeest as he can cover a dry terrain with ease. He is a largish member of the antelope breed, but not as big as the eland and quite a sight, so the term 'bump into' will be avoided. He, however, has the distinction of a second name which can redeem and make up for the rather rude descriptions he can be unkindly given like 'ugly'. His other simple nomenclature is the gnu, pronounced according to the *Oxford English Dictionary* as 'noo'. This rhymes with 'boo', and he may give you a surprise with his serious brow and intelligent, you could say learned, look. The female too, of course! Michael Flanders and Donald Swann introduced a musical ballad on his subject, giving a different pronunciation for his popular name which has somewhat taken off through the words, "I'm a g-nu, a g-nother g-nu". Thanks to this ditty, he has lightened up, metaphorically speaking, and raises a humorous smile.

The gnu has a multitude of relations, including the delightful and graceful gazelle. You may cross paths with a Thompson's or Grant's gazelle. Either has become an almost incongruous reminder for Brits of home in some of these deserted patches, though numerous outsiders did aid in saving their kind. Then also there is the Springbok which is hard to dissociate from fleet-footed South African footballers. Another small, agile member of the clan is the impala, of which there are quantities in the playground of Ray.

When the midday sun gets really blazing, the elephants take a break. The little one notices in the distance some human activity. There is a minibus full of visitors 'on safari'. They have stopped a few paces away from the attraction, to admire a group of zebras (or zebra) whose riveting stripes of black and white against yellow sand will always draw the eye. Their tails, like many others, flick. Stacks and sacks will be the postcards winging their way overseas tonight, demonstrating this unparalleled phenomenon which is said to enable swift adaptation between warmth and coolness. The sharp contrast of colour is clearly their winning badge.

Dramatically, a lioness appears from cover. Impalas skip and jump in every direction, dead set on escaping her intent. She is by nature carnivorous and cannot help it. You would surely forgive her if you could see her two enchanting offspring. Her cubs are playing together outside the den, their little pink noses not fully red yet and their tasselled tails dancing against the blue sky, just so. Next the king of beasts himself, in other words a lion, leaving aside pride is heard. His fine roar will be registered, but he is not too loud. His mighty, maned majesty may brush the brink shortly, but not yet. A pack of wild dogs chips in, not playing dummy and out of warren.

A capable also-ran member of the cat family somewhere about is the cheetah, who is the fastest of all animals. When one shows up, he is likely to get up speed, but it is difficult for a streaking specimen to alter direction quickly, as any potential quarry soon discovers. Dodges for bolting must be perfected to beat the competition. All, in need, do exercise some quality. Even the grunting warthogs have spunk.

The lofty crew can be oblivious to this movement. They soon progress into the afternoon shift, once the hot sun has passed maximum. With many near misses and close shaves round their sensitive steps, they observe shadows lengthening, their eyes topping high grains. An advancing watch it is. One more day is finally nearing its end. Ample welcoming splashes have been done and the temperature lowers. The heavens glow. Evening and winsome twilight are relished and lost. Booming and bellowing have diminished and changed key. But life goes on here purposefully.

A leopard is climbing down off a thick tree trunk. It is a female who has her young infant, masculine as it happens, up on a substantial branch. Curiosity will not kill this cat. Nor is she likely to change her velvet spots or even fade them. She has her thoughts fully engaged, and there is no need to say how or where. The darkness she considers a protection, though her colouring shimmers in the moonlight.

The elephant crowd is not far away. Some of them may yet use their weight to bring down a tree or two, probably out of sight of most, but not necessarily of the ranger in his Land Rover. Relationships, nevertheless, in spite of mutual games of eye-spying, are passable on both sides. Maybe these necessarily well-rounded beasts will have the chance to supplement their intake by extracting some more fruit and nuts, crushing any shells for the kernels under their formidable feet, used for purposes of distant contact through vibrations too.

Their circuit is nearly complete and they can go to sleep satisfied. They do sometimes vary their route considerably, always under the guidance of grandmother who knows the countryside thoroughly, but not so inside-out as the meerkats!. When Ray is a little older their party will be climbing single-file to higher ground where, from a cave, they will be able to withdraw some salt. Without being told, they know the wisdom of this extracted ingredient which, for men and women as well, is a buffer against excessive heat.

Tonight the stars shine and the air is reasonably cooler, refreshing our elephant assembly. There are several dozen buffalo who have settled almost on their normal bed-time site. No one need worry long-term about their presence. By morning all have vanished in their desire for fresh feeding grounds, solely leaving behind masses of hoof marks in the dust, the size of nursery plates. Elephants can sleep upright. They wake restored, anyway.

So the summer moves on again, fortunately not too eventfully for the elephants, who search the sky¬line above the long grass. Quite likely soon there will be a trumpeting blast and the male mob, with their incontestable white ivory tusks, will put in an appearance and socialize. It will only be a shotgun affair but certainly one to be reckoned with, in view of impact and other considerations! Any pregnancies resulting would last out the next year. However, nothing in that line of thought is transpiring at present. All is lulled in the every-day.

*   *   *

It was just at the time of a typical morning pool dip that a little occurrence, definitely unexpected, did take place. Free from patronizing twists, Ray and Will had wiggled their ears at each other in their customary style of greeting and, after moseying on down for refreshment, entered the water together. Two flashy birds with striking green feathers were perched among the twigs and branches of an adjacent tree, making a great deal of noise, in fact a din, as though they were showing off their wares, or perhaps one should say 'wears'. Whether Will got distracted or not, as he could do, the next thing Ray knew, his mate had done a disappearing act and members of his party, the whole company, were retreating.

It was exactly at this minute that Ray realized he was standing where a hippo had previously been and the resulting mud slack was sinking beneath him. Eyes were watching him from the closest bush growth on scrubland. It was the crouch of the striped hyenas, who always managed to be not far away when anything was going on. They are reputed to have a laugh like humans, but who would want any 'ha ha' now, let alone shrill like theirs. It was no laughing matter.

A voluble noise could simultaneously be heard from the nearest wooded copse. There to be seen were monkeys exhibiting their swinging dexterity up in the canopy. With such talent they might be skilled and regarded as a brainy family unit, but they were no use to our plighted poppet. Nor were any of the poor ostriches in line formation on the horizon who, fast as they frequently are, only get accused of putting their head in the sand when an emergency problem looms or arises. Sight drew a blank there, as previously over the sundrily assorted arena.

In this balanced though chancy existence and changeable environment, wonderfully help proved to be at hand. Some antelopes happened to be approaching the crease and one, in exuberance, was skipping ahead of the rest of the bunch. His youth gave him plenty of natural bounce and inquisitiveness so that he could understand the predicament. Without delay he entered the water and gave Ray a gentle push, that is to say shove from behind. Now you might think that such a slender animal could not make much impression, but his long thin legs and light weight enabled him not to slip down too far in the muddy depths.

Moreover, you have no doubt already contemplated the straw that broke the camel's back. In short, that little amount of pressure just made all the difference, and the baby elephant was quickly out on the shore strip by the rising bank and heading for his mother, who was not far away but anxious that she had let him stray, even with Will, more than a trunk length's distance away from her. Aunts and cousins crowded round and ensured that everything was back to normal and plain sailing or, rather, plodding pads, in no time.

Summer weather hung on spasmodically with ins and outs until there were ten days running of exceptionally high temperatures. The elephants, like all inhabitants of this establishment, wanted to go continuously to one of the water holes, which, needless to say, were all becoming jammed and low in supply. So it was not altogether surprising when another small incident took hold at the opposite end of the spectrum.

The elephant contingent was stepping to a sunken spot for dampening renewal when Ray pinpointed, to one side, an animal lying prostrate. It was an antelope who had succumbed to the excessive heat and collapsed. There could be no atom of shade for him since there were no trees. Our hero did not hesitate or lose a moment in coming to the rescue. He hotfooted at once to the edge of the shallows, filled his trunk with H_2O and showered it over the patient.

Massive dehydration gradually began to disappear. An ear twitched and next the tail flipped. As the elephants departed after their dip, it was completely reassuring to see the antelope upright and seeking relief in submergence. Had this been his pal in adversity? In any case, one good deed deserves another. Everybody was satisfied.

Forward the seasons displayed their usual fluctuations with ups and downs, and life went on its way with accustomed sensual animus. Ray, before long, was getting noticeably expansive. He was leaving baba antics behind though not the possibility of emulating the adored

French character in print, Babar. He might indeed one day become lord of the domain. It was on the cards, definitely on line to happen, as you might say. But for the present Ray was still learning from the sundry lessons of this cradle continent. He retained the memorable events in his maturing mind of growing scale, because, of course, an elephant never forgets!

*   *   *

If you believe this last section more readily than the opening one, dream on!

John Cabot
1450 - 1498

It was 'Henry the Navigator'(1394-1460) who aroused the European curiosity in exploring distant lands. He was the fourth son of John I of Portugal and he had an English mother, which has always been taken to have had an influence on his sea-faring fascination. Both west into the Atlantic and south-east round the coast of Africa, the first charts are Portuguese. Compatriot Vasco da Gama (1469-1524) extended the range past the Cape of Good Hope.

Christopher Columbus (1451-1506) used these charts for the Atlantic, though he was actually supported by King Ferdinand and Queen Isabella of Spain. His initial journey to the Caribbean was on the *Santa Maria* in 1492, and he continued looking for a spice route and founding trading colonies. He had spent some early years in Genoa as did John Cabot, or Caboto in its Italian form, who had been born there, the latter youth being just one year older if records accurate. Thus their lives had similarities.

John Cabot moved over to Venice and even got to Mecca, the heart of the spice trade, so important in the need for the preservation of food. What he saw increased his desire to find a north-west passage via the Atlantic. Hence his approach to King Henry VII of England. The King was far-seeing enough to agree to back him. Cabot only got one ship, the *Matthew,* and eighteen men, who included his three sons. They set sail in May 1497 and landed on Cape Breton Island the following month, unfurling the King's standard. Some of his naming revealed the Christian man. They reached Bristol again early in August.

The next year they went a second time with a larger contingent. They spent longer on the North American mainland which confirmed the position they hold as the first Europeans to officially touch ground on the continent. Cabot may have thought like Columbus that he had reached Asia, but then the natives were basically of Asian descent. Cabot's men noted the fish and furs as they went down the coast, going on into warmer temperatures, though soon returned to England, where it has to be admitted people seemed to lose momentum on the subject. No further trips were organized during the two reigns of the Henrys, but they both increased the strength of the naval fleet. John Cabot is thought to have died amongst his family, on the final voyage,but many facts in his life remain sketchy and uncertain.

America, rather by chance, came to be named after Amerigo Vespucci, a Florentine who came to Seville to help with the shipbuilding, and he accompanied some of the navigators, writing so-called letters describing the adventures. He had put portions of his own money into the Atlantic affair, with surveys right down the eastern seaboard, so perhaps the naming was justified.

If you look, you can find a plethora of earlier tales of discovery. Forget about the Irish St Brendan who was mainly on a spiritual mission, the Welsh prince who took a party up from Florida trailing a corricle boat for the Spanish to find, the Venetian Zen brothers curious to go north. Facts can be refuted or fuzzed as fantasy. The Vikings did leave a late-medieval date carved on stone over by the Great Lakes, and the Chinese, sailing from the east, are said to have found routes and possess a map. How about Erik the Red in the Icelandic Sagas eyeing the coast by Vineland? The title America was put on a map and accepted by the majority, finally being legalized. End of story.

The people of England finally recognized the importance of Cabot in launching their initial exploration leading to empire and eventual commonwealth. In 1897 a tall tower was erected to honour him in Bristol, his port of departure.

Francis Drake
circa 1545 – 1596

This very famous Englishman, particularly so in his day, was born in Devon and soon felt the lure of the nearby sea, which never left him. He learnt most of his seamanship from his cousin, Captain John Hawkins (1532-95), a bit of a freebooter while also establishing the navy with his ships. Some may call Drake a pirate, at best a publicist, though he was much more than that if one considers the contemporary situation. Americans and others may kid you about piracy, but you should not take it too seriously.

Spain reneged on a naval truce, attacking English ships, and had also threatened to invade England on behalf of the Catholic Church. Then, Queen Elizabeth I and her supporters were Protestant, so Drake no doubt too felt he was defending freedom and right. These were fluctuating and rather unpredictable times in various ways for his country, as for many.

He was a plucky, shortish man with red hair, which is a form of fairness. After the Spanish attack, Drake took himself off on his ship, now named the *Golden Hind*. He rounded Cape Horn and entered the Pacific, travelling right up the coast as far as the north of Canada, plundering a Spanish ship on the way. During the early part of the sixteenth century Spain had been free without competition to establish colonies and to extort gold.

The English now were concentrating interests on looking for the North-west Passage. Martin Frobisher (1535-94) tried from the eastern side. Drake meanwhile was also hampered by ice, the sea unpropitious. On his way down the western side, when eventually reaching the south again, he stopped at some spice islands. Afterwards, rather than face the Spaniards in the Atlantic, he took the momentous decision to turn westwards, thus circumnavigating the globe. He had no charts to guide him, only his simple compass and the stars.

The Portuguese Ferdinand Magellan (1480-1521) had been credited with the first such trip. Yes, our world was round, if anyone still doubted it! The crew had suffered hardship, reduced at one stage, we are told, to eating the ship's leather, which is certainly grim but perhaps heroic as well. Then Magellan himself, who was sailing for the Spaniards, got killed in a Pacific skirmish, and the ship came home without him in 1521. So Francis Drake was the first leader to live to tell the tale. Queen Elizabeth knighted him on his ship at his return in 1580 after three years.

In 1587 Drake led a raid on Cadiz to attack the Spanish shipping, claiming thereby to have singed the King of Spain's beard. The English had been dreading an attack, and the next year, 1588, the Spanish Armada arrived. Philip II intended to overrun England but the ships were harried from behind and in other ways which, with the stormy windy weather, destroyed notions of conquest. Many of the enemy ships were wrecked off Scotland. Of those Spaniards who made it round to western Ireland, some stayed there as witness the Spanish Arch in Galway Bay.

The favourite anecdote which has come down to us from the Spanish Armada is that Drake was playing bowls on Plymouth Ho and remarked, 'There is time to finish the game and beat the Spaniards too!' What can be said to be without doubt true is that such a stance would capture the spirit of this courageous and brilliant buccaneer. Plymouth Ho is situated on raised ground with a magnificent view of the natural harbour. On a summer evening the exit west with the glow of a setting sun is most inviting. It is exactly from this place in 1620 that the Pilgrim Fathers and Mothers set sail in the *Mayflower*. Their names are listed against the rock by the water's edge; but this adventure was still in the future, that is to say the following century.

Francis Drake continued to voyage. The hot climate, particularly in that epoch of early travel, was difficult. He died off Panama, and near the Caribbean Islands, even on that final expedition penetrating on foot into Mexico. He considered the world, if not his oyster, at least open to everyone, and this enabled the English to see it that way as far as the oceans were concerned. The large, ample home which Drake bought for himself in Devonshire was Buckfast Abbey. There is now a permanent exhibition at this site, which can be inspected, displaying artefacts and memorabilia in his name.

Walter Raleigh
1552 - 1618

Here is another renowned adventurer and explorer who also possessed many other talents. He was born in south Devon to a gentleman landowner who had fallen on hard times. Walter attended Oriel College, Oxford, for a period. He then joined an army campaign helping the Huguenots in France against the Catholics. He was also to spend some time in Ireland. It becomes clear finally that, like Drake, Raleigh responded to the tang of the sea.

He is remembered with delight for his, so claimed, gallant action at Greenwich when he threw down his cloak so that the Queen did not have to step in the mire. He quickly became one of Queen Elizabeth's favourites and was painted by several artists including the miniaturist Nicholas Hilliard. One can see he too had a red touch, though slight, added to his darkish hair, and he was a good-looking man, so that you could feel, in many respects, he was commendable.

Walter was the son of his father's third wife. He had an older half-brother, Humphrey Gilbert (1539-83), who had already aroused the country to interests in distant lands through his seaward expeditions. Walter inherited when his brother's ship went down and, with his close relationship by the Queen, he was able to further England's capacity in that direction, developing considerable naval know-how.

In 1584 he was knighted and became Sir Walter Raleigh, thus acquiring a soubriquet to suit his dignity and bearing. He was responsible for naming his country's first American territory Virginia in the Queen's honour. This was a stretch of land extending beyond the present state borders to much wider boundaries, which could be somewhat ill-defined and competitive.

In the year 1585 he raised money towards the initial expedition for settlement in America at Roanoke under his cousin Richard Grenville. Unfortunately, despite further efforts, this was not a permanent endeavour, though it had two immediate effects. Sir Walter brought back from the colony to Europe the first potatoes as a vegetable and tobacco, which was used for smoking by the native Americans in their peace-pipes and such like. The puffing habit gradually grew in England, not being far-reaching at first. Now it has retreated again.

Raleigh, in due course, in spite of some success, lost favour with the Queen when he wooed and then married Elizabeth Frogmorton, one of her Maids of Honour which was forbidden. He spent much of the rest of his life in the Tower of London. He was no mean writer of verse and of treatises, and while there also started what was planned to be quite an extensive 'History of the World'. With the Stuarts coming to the throne, he thought it might receive royal patronage for family use.

He did in his last year make one more trip to the New World. This was to South America, where he had previously shown kindness to natives, in search of gold on behalf of James I, who had become King of England and Scotland in 1603. The journey, not unexpectedly at that stage, was fruitless, and Sir Walter was beheaded soon after his return. It was an age needing courage, which this hero certainly possessed. You will find people now who will say he lost his head in revenge for Queen Elizabeth's beheading of James's mother, Mary Queen of Scots.

There was another English explorer who became active early in the seventeenth century and would end with his name on the maps, that was Henry Hudson (1565-1611). Hudson Bay in northern Canada, where the Hudson Bay Company still exists, was named for him, as was the Hudson River, flowing down New York State to the west of Manhattan. The latter naming was because he prospected with physical-feature mapping for the Dutch in 1610, resulting their succesful claim. Walter Raleigh helped lay the foundations for future success.

In eventual distribution, Sir Walter Raleigh's own extended colonial area to the south became part of the state of North Carolina, and its capital town, Raleigh, named after him. It continues so today, with regard to both state and capital. At Sherborne, Dorset, in England the cherished mansion with garden, which Queen Elizabeth gave to Raleigh while he was in favour, still stands.

James Cook
1728 – 1779

Exploration and European settlement moved fast, and so there was a somewhat different picture when James Cook arrived on the scene, but still with much to be discovered. He was born in a Yorkshire village on 28 October 1728; so he was born in the same county as Martin Frobisher, though the family of the earlier navigator had originally come from Wales. As a youth James Cook, before long, found himself working for some ship owners in Whitby, Scandinavians who ran a service to the continent across the uncertain North Sea. He grew to over six foot.

In his twenties Cook joined the Royal Navy, and he was soon doing some surveying work on the St Lawrence River in eastern Canada. He was noted as a good mathematician and astronomer, and, when the time came, he was selected to command the *Endeavour* which was travelling with such passengers and luminaries as the naturalist Joseph Banks to observe Venus eclipse the sun in the South Pacific. They also surveyed the coasts of New Zealand and Australia, which resulted in these places becoming ultimately part of the British Empire. Certainly these regions had previously been visited by Dutch and Portuguese vessels. The journey round the world took three years for Captain Cook and party, 1768-71, and they brought back new plant specimens, as Charles Darwin would later on the *Beagle*.

Cook spent ten years in his travels, a long time, making two more trips to the Pacific where in the first he actually went down as far as Antarctica and he also explored Tahiti and located other islands. Interest in the possible North-west Passage had not abated. In his final voyage he surveyed up the western coast of America until blocked by ice beyond the Arctic Circle, and then came down on the Chinese side, taking in various points of Asia. Only in 2007 did global warming open up the route north of Canada.

Returning back south he stopped again in Hawaii where he had been before, and there a most unfortunate event occurred. Following a dispute over one of his boats, Cook disembarked and went among the natives where he was killed. This was a sad end for a humane married man.

As matters went, the tragedy did nothing to stop heroic adventure. During the nineteenth century, in the year 1847, John Franklin tried to make a sea voyage from the Atlantic north of Canada and was not heard of again. Late in the next century traces of the expedition were still coming to light but mystery remains. The cutting-edge of exploration moved on to the poles where there have been compelling trekking tales. 'Scott of the Antarctic' and his bonded breed of companions, in their plight, plucked the heart strings of national sensibilities. Scott had followed Ernest Shackleton (1874-1922), Irish born, who also achieved famed exploits in this freezing zone.

Patriotism may next have looked elsewhere, as to Lawrence of Arabia, who, in his original striving beyond the norm, manages to finish by being crowned with romantic zeal. Bravery boundaries subsequently expanded to the ocean floor and then to the realms of outer space, which, drawing on the assistance of satellites, has been the new frontier. Scientific inventions can reduce risks to life itself, but the human race continues to accept challenge.

There was a somewhat unusual little incident, which might finally be mentioned in connection with Captain James Cook. He did like to befriend people, and on one of his journeys to Tahiti his group picked up a young man who was keen to come and see England. The Tahitan's name was Omai. He joined one of Cook's ships and reached what proved to be welcoming shores in 1774. He was taken up by high society whose members were fascinated in him, and even got his portrait painted by Sir Joshua Reynolds. After two years he returned home, which was probably the sensible thing for him to do; but do not imagine that such a person would not be acceptable in Britain at the time.

What to Expect

The United States is now regarded as the world's super-power though with less certainty as many other countries make valuable contributions and all regard themselves in some way superior. In view of America's dominance, particularly for the western world, it is worth taking the country truly on board if you can, that is to say making a personal-experience visit. One needs to get beyond the coke, popcorn and hotdog. In this section 'we' is used sometimes to guide above all the so-termed British like myself, but it is written for all to ponder, even if solely in an armchair. Any new variance points up a changing culture.

At first, on arrival, everything may seem very big and immensely strange. The traffic in its wide swathes, moves in the opposite direction from Britain, which must not be forgotten. Cross at the corners or you may be had up for jay-walking! The language, probably with relief, is manageable in spite of differences which may trip one, as for instance in the pharmacy or drugstore, not chemist, one must remember that to ask for paper handkerchiefs is likely to get you nowhere! If in some store, favoured over shop, you cannot serve yourself, ask for Kleenex, brand name, or tissues. Should you want some drawing pins, say thumb tacks. There are variations too, like 'first floor' for the ground floor, elevator for lift, but you can get used to them, and basically one is grateful for the English tongue most of the time, even with foxing accents.

Of course, American films, in all their variety, have got one accustomed to some slang. Petrol being gasoline, there is the catch-phrase 'step on the gas' for speed. In punctuation, 'period' is used for `fullstop', providing such idioms as, 'That is the situation, period.' In other words, there is nothing more to be said. To call may mean to visit, not phone, and to be smart most likely clever. With regard to spelling, Noah Webster (1758-1843), of dictionary recall, has been responsible for much of the standardization over there, supposedly to simplify. Then there is zee for zed, but nothing beyond what can be sorted as with the venerated *Uncle Remus and Br'er Rabbit* of Joel Chandler Harris (1848-1908).

Often one feels people forget that many Americans, even today, are mainly from the same stock. It is possible, and quite probable, that you have some relations there. Your family surname may appear on a sign-post or come to you elsewhere. When reading a short history of the U.S.A. I found that in an early industrial dispute, the management side was led by someone with my paternal grandmother's maiden name and the workers side by someone with my maternal grandmother's maiden name! Such are the coincidences one can find. In other words we are all not so different as is often made out and can benefit from mutual contact and influence.

However, since the Revolutionary War of 1775 we have grown apart. You may feel called upon to justify what the British did, since one does become a representative of the homeland whenever one travels and, on the reverse side, gets reflected glory from anything achieved, even the previous week. You could, for instance, be admired for motor-racing though you have never been to a track!

The War of Independence can crop up in different ways. On a guided tour of Boston it may be pointed out that the metal balconies were made from English guns and cannon. Do not be phased. It is worth coming to grips a bit with that war, which for English people may be just one of many. The British Empire, which Americans took against, was intended primarily for trade, and we were very busy at the moment of the American events with promoting our imports of such items as spices, cloth and tea from India, not to mention sugar from the Caribbean. Then, too, numerous British citizens who were trading with America, had lived there for a period, or had relations across the sea. While others, in view of the size of the Atlantic, were a bit indifferent to what went on that far away. Perhaps, above all, there were those uneasy about fighting our own former compatriots on racial or religious grounds.

Many on the colonial side felt similarly, and one can read much into the facts of thousands who moved up to Canada to stay together with us. Probably there were more in America who felt rather ambivalent but did not uproot. It is worth recalling these factors when considering Britain's sensible decision not to pursue the conflict further. The same set of facts can be viewed from diverse angles, as those of us privileged to learn this stretch of history in schools on both sides of the divide can testify!

To advance a few decades, if history has not been your *forte,* you might be surprised to be told on a visit to the White House in Washington, that the British had sacked the building in 1814. This was two years into the War of 1812. It is true that fighting did break out again between us in that year but the Americans will readily admit that mistakes were made on both sides, forays into Canada getting a mention.

Since the Second World War our two countries have become much closer together. Radio and television have contributed to this and, as you might say too, the shrinking of the world. In the big picture we divided into the eastern and western blocks, and London gradually increased its awareness of the importance of Washington, giving us more coverage about the U.S. generally. Many in our country can think back to the tension that built up and was firmly in place by the sixties. So it was for Great Britain, as well as America, a fantastic experience when, one Friday work day, information seeped through that President Kennedy had been shot. We were a bit like pig-in-the-middle, with all that fearful anticipation and uncertainty of the era suddenly released. The different countries had to continue to grapple with any fall-out after the assassination and move lives along, but it was almost as though our planet had been stunned and wavered for a moment.

General Douglas MacArthur, who became a national icon of the twentieth century, warned the American people not to get drawn into a ground war in south-east Asia. That is just what happened in Vietnam, resulting in their troops finally leaving without victory. Americans always liked to say they had never lost a war, but now, in spite of some heroic actions, they were joining the crowd. Such things are surmountable.

These days one cannot end a piece on America without mentioning the 2001 destruction of the 110-storey twin-towers in lower Manhattan New York, the spot now christened, or tagged, as 'Ground Zero'. Never before had the country suffered a comparable catastrophe on its own soil. The action gave a new dimension to the problems of the world, and the United States in particular. Its happening became known as 9/11, which does point up one more little variation with the old country needing to be absorbed. The Americans always put the month before the day in abbreviating dates, thus eleventh of September. The empty space did, however, offer site for new inspirational Freedom Tower.

It can be fruitless to use the word Empire in connection with the Americans because they like to consider their country stands for freedom against empire, even though of course most English people in the modern world were glad for the British Empire to become a commonwealth for sharing. Developments in 2003 and after brought the British and U.S. military even closer together, strengthening our contacts. Through financial dealings we have all relied a little bit on Uncle Sam, and increasingly so with global integration, interjected with credit crunch.

To be with Americans can give one a sense of completion since they are an English-speaking society, and therefore inevitably with much in common. The United States has long had the name John or Jane Doe to represent their average anonymous American, which is especially used in legal jargon. You may find you never quite get to the bottom of what the Americans feel in respect to their opinion of the English. Let that be. They are sure to be very welcoming and friendly to our lot, being unexpectedly traditional in many ways themselves, and in something of an anomaly, admire the Royal Family with their appreciation of quality and success. When a wedding comes, 'the British know how to put on a good show.' So enjoy yourself, and revel in the relaxed optimism which you are certain to still note there in America.

Florida

The Spanish were the first Europeans credited with a landing on the peninsula of Florida, calling it thus because it was Easter time and they were struck by the rich array of exotic flowers, in fact flora and fauna in abundance. Christopher Columbus had noticed in the Caribbean waters the manatees, or sea-cows, which he thought initially looked like frolicking mermaids because of their fish-like tails and large heads. The alligators, draping moist banks of Florida, were slightly smaller than their African cousins, the crocodiles.

To start with, the Spaniards made no settlements. After all, there were people already in residence who were happy without new-comers. These natives did, however, bring up to manhood a cabin boy who was the only survivor of a shipwrecked Spanish galleon. He was in fact not reunited with his own kind for many years, which was a unique experience.

Fact can easily get mixed with fiction. It is said that Pizarro, the best known of the Conquistadors, chased a pretty native damsel up a tree. She, in her keenness to get away, stepped out on a branch and nimbly lowered herself to the ground. Pursuing, Pizarro found his part in the escapade more difficult, stumbled along the bough and then caught his beard in the descent. That became the start of Spanish moss, which now decks the woodlands of Florida so charmingly!

In 1539 Hernando De Soto left a garrison in the area and then in 1565 the first permanent Spanish mission was founded in St Augustina on the north-eastern coast below Jacksonville, and now considerably reconstructed like Williamsburg in Virginia. It contains one of the claimants to be the oldest colonial house still standing in America. There is also a well positioned fort overlooking a natural harbour. Even on hot sunny afternoons the Spaniards must have kept a watchful eye for any shipping passing by, be it Dutch, French,

English or other, among increasing operations, leaving aside the Pacific coast of the continent where, before the end of the sixteenth century, the Spanish were in addition exploring.

Then in 1819, after a somewhat chequered period, Florida was purchased from the Spaniards by the United States. Florida was before long drained and a highway driven through, leading to the present extension and network of roads but with some characteristic swampy places retained. There are marinelands too these days with fishy aquariums and performing porpoises.

Continuing southwards down the coast one reaches the Kennedy Space Center at Cape Canaveral, part of NASA. Many unprecedented journeys have started here, perhaps none causing more awe than the early Apollo missions. One eye-witness who turned up intending to protest on some issue, said that when the spaceship soared up in the air, 'Man, I just stood and stared', overcome with the excitement and wonder of it all! He was just proud to be an American.

Slightly westwards towards the centre of the state is Orlando, the landing-point for numerous holiday-makers flying in to experience the Disney World theme park, which now covers over one hundred square miles. Within is a wild-life park in addition to a multitude of novel rides and entertainments. There is sure to be a rollercoaster for a flutter which, needless to say, will be, well, big. Walt Disney (1901-66) has long been an international symbol of America with his unique collection of stylized animals. It is reported that when he originally thought of doing a cat after Felix, his wife suggested a mouse. Certainly a happy conjunction anyway was to arrive at the creation of Mickey. For the military, Donald Duck in his naval cap has a special ranking. Each of us can choose a favourite. What is assured is that countless British fans have taken Disney World to their hearts.

Advancing nearer towards the foot of Florida is Palm Beach, always a popular spot for Americans. Then comes Miami, the big draw. Canadians too, when the cold weather arrives, like to have a *pied à terre* down there. Summers can get very tricky in the coastal cantons. This may be the 'Sunshine State' but one must be guarded about the July to October typhoon syndrome, that is to say, hurricane season. Such caution applies to the milder westerly seaboard as well, where St Petersburg is nevertheless a top-class haven.

Further down the western side on the Gulf of Mexico are the Everglades, a penetrating section to experience by boat. Some of the Seminole Indians, native to the region, live here. I do hope they do not object to my designating them an Indian tribe. I find the name attractive and fascinating with its own history. Who can think of the plains Indian chiefs in feathered finery without responding to the title? Red Indian from skin tone was, of course, long accepted for native American.

Now at the tip of the state we reach Key West, a highly valued destination not to be overlooked. Here Ernest Hemmingway (1898-1961), a literary leader and personality, in fact giant of his time, liked to relax. Some compatriots favour other locations, but Florida in its vitality should not be ignored. Storms have increased to include violent tornadoes, so you need to check timing and take care.

The capital is Tallahassee, worthily remembered in song, and situated right up close to the border with Georgia, a state of the Deep South, and which was also the home of Margaret Mitchell (1900-49) who only wrote one novel, *Gone with the Wind*. In 1939 the famous film of the book was released with English actress Vivien Leigh as Scarlet opposite heartthrob Clark Gable, and featuring too in this southern spellbinder English charmer Leslie Howard. Winding on, to the end of this four-hour flick, 'Tomorrow is another day!' So it is for Florida, with happy hordes as supplement pouring in from abroad, many even seeking their own dream home with pool.

Boston

The Mayflower duly arrived in America towards the end of the year 1620. Though not originally seeking so northerly a situation the Pilgrims descended at Plymouth, the exact rock they alighted upon now commemorated. This was the first permanent English settlement because 1607 Jamestown had not survived. The new arrivals numbered just over one hundred, but nearly half of them died during the initial harsh winter and were buried on the hillside by their ancient church.

Salem, along the shore-line to the north on Massachusetts bay, was founded nine years later, by which time many boats were coming, plying their way almost three thousand miles. Then, the following year, in 1630, John Winthrop turned up with seven hundred souls, choosing the fortuitous site of Boston just below, but above Plymouth. This section became much favoured, and the population has continued to grow swiftly ever since.

The Irish have found the town a convenient place, and not too distant, to congregate, including members of the Kennedy clan, but there is no need for fairy-tales here. The land is full of myths and legends, centring above all on the Boston Tea Party and all its ramifications. The wharf is still there for inspection. Ruby Wax, at one of gracious Queen Elizabeth II's Golden Jubilee Concerts in the grounds of Buckingham Palace, commented, reassuring for the senior descendent of George III, that 'the tea party' was 'a joke'. Nice to know that! The inhabitants of Boston and region in the late eighteenth century had grown to about fifteen thousand people.

Across the wide Charles River is the town of Cambridge with the first American University, a foundation dating from 1636. The two towns have always been in close proximity not just physically, and inevitably more so in the early days. The university was named after John Harvard, a graduate of Emmanuel College, Cambridge in England, where his name is perpetuated. He gave a large bequest to the university on his death, having lived in the colony, and the connection also resulted in the new town becoming Cambridge. Initialled M.I.T. and more would follow later. Other universities gradually grew up in the eastern states, notably Yale and Princeton, all of which acquired the communal name of Ivy League, holding their prestige against more modem state universities for many years to come. It has been said that in America the universities contain the cream of society. Some assuredly would dispute this.

There is no doubt that to begin with the Boston area embraced the hub of intellectual and literary life. Ralph Waldo Emerson (1803-82) became a premier philosopher and essayist. Nathaniel Hawthorne (1704-64) a century earlier had built an international reputation with *The Scarlet Letter* and composing many stories such as *Twice-Told Tales*. He was born and lived much in Salem, the formerly bewitched but now peaceful historic town. His home is a brief walk from the water's edge where the shipping came and went. Henry Wadsworth Longfellow (1807-82) was born in Portland, Maine, but came to live in an imposing house within the verdant suburbs of Cambridge. He is renowned above all for 'The Song of Hiawatha', a mythic narrative poem. All these three writers were familiar, through their voyaging, with Britain and, across the Channel, the continent of Europe. The crossing of the Atlantic in the eighteenth century could still take six weeks, gradually dropping in the nineteenth century with the advanced clippers, and finally being reduced dramatically with the coming of iron-clad steam ships.

A disciple of Emerson, through his interest in mysticism, was Henry Thoreau (1817-62). He was born in Concord, another early town, a little inland from Boston. Representing the womenfolk of America was the much loved novelist Louisa May Alcott (1832-88), famous for *Little Women, Jo's Boys* and other titles. Though born in Philadelphia, she was raised for the most part in Concord. Her pretty house, quite near the roadside, can readily be seen to this day. The white clapboard houses, typical of New England usually with porches and contrasting painted shutters, have survived well. You may enter one, constructed long ago, with an upstairs plan and latch doors very like some in East Anglia, which is the side of England from which most of the first settlers came. Boston, in fellow-feeling, is named after the eastern town of Lincolnshire. As the communities spread and moved inland the prototype Main Street developed, with often a becoming white, spired Congregational church. Such a sight fascinates the tourist, especially when autumn colours emerge in the Fall on the bountiful syrup-tapped, red-leaved maple trees, heralding Halloween. If the weather is mild late, the term 'Indian Summer' tends to get an airing.

The sea-scape boroughs around Boston can be a draw, with plentiful lobsters and clam-chowder soup. High on the cliffs stand the whalers' mansions, perhaps in yellow with black shutters, a popular combination. In the bay at Marblehead are the sailing boats, early tombs not far away. The climate of New England provides snow and ice for skiing and skating in the winter and hot sun for camping and swimming in the summer. The harsh conditions are epitomized by John Greenleaf Whittier (1807-92) in his poem 'Snowbound' and the contrasting settled heat in 'The Barefoot Boy' with cheek of tan. Children dream of their long vacation with a spell quite likely on the coast of Maine or Cape Cod. This is maybe their ideal. Moreover, they have learnt the history and know that Boston is the centre of the world! That is what can be felt.

It is a draw, being more than just the capital of Massachusetts. Its innate quality maintains its distinction. Though on the bay, it is centrally placed for New England. Much of the style of the buildings in the Old Town, as at Harvard Yard, is clearly Colonial Georgian. Newbury Street, the shopping Promenade and winding roads nearby, can be reminiscent of England, some may feel most affecting in the softening evening light. On Beacon Hill, the terraced houses and period lamp-standards are visually absorbing. The English might have lost out, but one can still read occasionally of claims for compensation. This place is nevertheless a New World town, and life will not stand rigid. The Hancock Tower is a demonstration of modernity. The name, however, draws one back again. You may too, after a roll-call of generations, come across a Reverend Brewster in the Church, or maybe on the street a present-day descendent of Miles Standish! To exalt the scope in architecture, continuous in the States, modem art has added riveting steel and glass to the waterfront.

The art galleries bear witness to a rich past. Among the most frequently reproduced pictures to be seen by local artists are those by James McNeill Whistler (1834-1903), though in fact he lived much abroad. Probably his most famous portrait of all was, rather unforeseenly therefore, that of his mother. This is all the more to be wondered at since it is said that he had intended at the time to paint a younger woman who had failed to turn up when awaited. Such an occurrence with its result shows how variable and unpredictable even success can be, emphasizing that one should assess as much as one is able personally. This picture representing maternal puritanism is in Paris. Perhaps on your walls once hung the coloured horses of Germany's Franz Marc (1880-1916). The original of his best known study in this line is on a wall in this cultural corner beside Boston. Quantities of recognizable classics share the hallowed ground.

Turning to music and finishing in a lighter strain for this primarily English settled area, one might pick out Cole Porter (1892-1964), actually from the rival establishment, Yale University to the south in New Haven, Connecticut (pronounced without the second 'c'). He was the universally acclaimed composer of the intrinsically American *Night and Day* and *In the Still of the Night*. So gradually more places of excellence developed. Members of Yale spoke of the need to equalize the law for all citizens long before it happened. As for ignorance over Jews, a picture of them having to leave their homes appeared on the front of 'The Times' close when war was declared. In the U.S., in 1941, a student told of an inmate who escaped from a ghastly Belsen. Finally action gave results.

There are six states altogether in New England. Rhode Island, with plenty of sandy beaches is on the south-east jagged rim. Pleasantly verdant New Hampshire is next to coastal Maine in the north, followed by hilly Vermont, sought for its ski runs. Every state has its individual as well as national identity.

New York

New Yorkers see where they are themselves as the centre of our modem world, and in many ways they are probably right! It is a great power-base with influence in multifarious fields, a metropolis not to be ignored. For smart getaway you could trip to Bermuda.

The days when the Dutch first arrived may seem unquestionably remote but the contribution of these pioneers to the town continues apparent, not least in nomenclature. Peter Minuit put down anchor in 1625, after the survey of 1624, with two hundred from Holland. It is no exaggeration that Manhattan was bought from the designated Indians for such items as beads and richly coloured cloth. Naturally all values were different in those days. One must not forget that. Peter Stuyvesant was sent over as Director-General of the Dutch colony in 1647 and he was responsible for the wall on the northern perimeter, still very much in proverbial down-town though they did have farms further afield. The wall may no longer stand, but the name Wall Street resulted and has been adopted by the hopefully humming financial sector. Remains can still be seen too of canals dug.

The British navy by the second half of the seventeenth century had become alert throughout the world. An advantageous exchange, as it turned out, was made with Holland by which New York was given over for a spice island in the southern seas. The inhabitants of what had been New Amsterdam accepted this. The English were already all around. Their ships came along the coast to land in 1664. Thus New York was born, but Stuyvesant had his name perpetuated in a local district. Some words of the Dutch language survive too. The noun 'stoop' is still employed to describe a flight of steps in front of a house such as a down-town brownstone. Even in contemporary life, someone from the eastern states will say that if, on a cloudy day, there is a patch of blue large enough to make a pair of Dutchman's breeches the sky will clear, and usually it does too!

Washington Irving (1783-1859) was fascinated by the Dutch tradition, writing about it in many ways. His most famous piece is *Rip van Winkle*, a folkloric tale about a settler who goes to sleep and wakes up years later when the world has changed for him. Irving lived along the Hudson River in a spot extremely like Sleepy Hollow, about which he also wrote. You could call it a rural idyll, and Walter Scott (1771-1832), who encouraged him in his endeavours, actually visited him there. A bevy of the nineteenth-century railway barons and similar men of wealth also chose this region for their mansions. West Point, the military academy is finely situated above the river. Up-state New York is altogether an attractive area for holidays, and the autumn always displays striking contrasts between the conifers and turning deciduous leaves on the hillsides. If, leaving Albany the capital well behind, and Woodstock of shared rap one goes all the way to the Canadian border, one can take in the Niagara Falls, generally considered most dramatic from the American side. A desirable destination for honeymooners, all of us must stand and wonder at the mighty flow of water passing every minute, viewed up or down with a splash.

Not unexpectedly, during the nineteenth century, thoughts in New York turned to the possibilities of bridge building. The result in 1883 was the opening of the much respected Brooklyn Bridge, designed by John Roebling. This linked Manhattan to Long Island and for years contained the longest suspension yet built. Walt Whitman (1819-92) in his poetic enthusiasm eulogized it. Many other gracious gateways followed, among them the Washington Bridge up by Riverside Drive . linking the west side to the mainland in New Jersey, and more modem still, the Verrazano Bridge, linking Brooklyn with Staten Island over the entrance to the harbour. At the birth of the twentieth century the Statue of Liberty, a gift from the French, was also in place on its islet to welcome new arrivals across the water. It can greet or bid farewell in its initial, or final, prominence.

Now the upward trend began with skyscrapers, not difficult to install on the hard rock of New York though in density a contribution to noise. The 'art deco' Chrysler Building, completed in 1930 with a shining spire, continues to be much admired, and the Empire State Building of the next year has been a magnet in its long-time dominance at 102 floors. The underground subway and expanding airports duly mushroomed.

After Greenwich Village, where artists and writers have liked to congregate, and New York University thrives, Fifth Avenue drives a central artery through the bourgeoned edifices, the numbered streets in regular sequence covering both east and west sides. There are many famous structures along this route, Rockefeller Center being a main focal point. It rose opposite the site of Saks, the department store, and a sunken ice-rink was introduced for the winter time. St Thomas's Church of the Episcopalian faith, in association with the Church of England, is as smart a place of worship as you can find anywhere, and the St Patrick's Roman Catholic Cathedral, on the other side of Fifth Avenue, has a natural prominence which draws the crowds. Tiffany's, the jewellery shop, is not far away for inspection.

The Museum of Modem Art in this area provides well attended exhibitions. Further up beyond the main entrance to Central Park at 59th Street is the all-embracing Metropolitan Museum of Art. To mention one other of many galleries, almost opposite is the Guggen-heim, which has an ascending spiral walkway of great originality.

All the arts, as is fully appreciated, are catered for magnificently on the west side, notably with Broadway lighted to dazzling point, the Great White Way. Many, pursuing drama, aspire to appear here. Arthur Miller, in his long life (1915-2005), often premiered in New York but was also known to choose England. Neil Simon is a playwright adept at sussing out his home town. There exists as well 'Off Broadway' for budding actors who sometimes end up as Hollywood film stars. The big Broadway shows are too numerous to call. Noel Coward (1899-1973) with Gertrude Lawrence in '*Private Lives*' can surface in recollections. Carol Channing was memorable in

'Hello Dolly', so appropriately about New York in New York. There is Radio City Music Hall with long reputation for cinema and a floor show.

Like the raised railway line, the old-style Metropolitan Opera House has become a nostalgic forerunner, albeit with great names like Caruso. The update was opened in 1966, joining the concert hall and the theatre at Lincoln Center. The Juilliard School of Music advances there with its own traditions, often accepting potential British soloists for some training, and the City Ballet progresses with its Balanchine credentials.

Some say Americans are too inclined to knock old buildings down, liking to quote the early car manufacturer, Henry Ford, in his dictum: 'History is bunk', though he did actually say 'more or less'. Carnegie Hall, with a face-lift perhaps, has presented musical performance for contemporaries right back to Tchaikovsky in the 1890s; even its name being redolent with associations and sentiment. Occasionally too, those who can afford the finance move whole buildings over from the old world, as for example in New York the French archaic relics now established at The Cloisters on a promontory at the top end of the island. Up-town also has Columbia University at 116 Street and near to 'Cotton Club' Harlem. Hopping over the water northwards, in the Bronx is the Yankie football stadium and the zoo. The best beaches are beyond fun-fair Coney Island on Long Island ending with the Hamptons, all valuable resorts since the air can get hot and humid. Apart from outdoor sports, a bowling alley will be squeezed in somewhere.

So the region provides endless pursuits and frequently expands through districts with delightful names like Yonkers and beyond. If you ever see the wide bands of gently advancing traffic after dark, it is an exhilarating eyeful! Vehicles circulate round and through the area all the time, because remember this is the place *par excellence* which never sleeps, and for the dedicated owls there will be night-clubs, some in familiar-sounding Soho. Joumalists among many will be working late, the *New Yorker* and *Time* magazines with venerable sites. Covering fashion, an important element in New York, there is at least one Institute and also a School of Design. Then for sporting events and large pageants which are not outdoors, like ticker-tape parades, there is Madison Square Garden.

An item on New York should not conclude before mentioning the United Nations headquarters, which is a large glass slab by the East River on First Avenue. Britain, accessing its wide and long legal experience, gives opinions received with respect. The complex can be reached from 42nd Street, a major crossway having an entrance to Grand Central Station and, on the west side, takes in Times Square. Yellow taxicabs are about if wanted, multi-coloured phase past.

You may find your aspirations have still not been touched on here. If that is the case it is more than likely some aspect of it can be found in this vibrant city, 'the big apple' as it has been long dubbed. One visitor from England described his experience as 'a dollar a breath'. It is true you may spend money, but in the atmosphere of this cosmopolitan creche and sophisticated sequel there is a pitched pad for all incomers. Not everyone aspires to stay in such as the immortalized Plaza Hotel, live in Brooklyn Heights, or have an apartment off Park Avenue with an awning and doorman. Reasonable places to stay can be tracked and the restaurants in their source-diversity and price-range are reassuring and inviting, therefore able to satisfy all the proverbial pockets.

Philadelphia

William Penn (1644-1718) became a Quaker in his youth and thereafter a keen advocate of religious freedom. In 1681 Charles II granted him land south of New York, and the following year he left England and arrived at his newly allocated acreage on the Delaware River. There was already a scattering of Dutch, Swedes and Finns in residence. These had been coming since the mid' seventeenth century, but only to rural areas and without much organization. They subsequently mingled with the new arrivals who continued to arrive in even greater numbers.

Penn established the territory as Pennsylvania, in memory of his father, and founded the first town which he called Philadelphia. The 'City of Brotherly Love' was well conceived and spaciously laid out with many trees which has given it to this day an elegant and distinguished air. In 1683 Penn signed a treaty of friendship with the Indians, so called, who also lived in the area. Its humane terms had long-standing and far-reaching effects.

Penn soon returned to England with one more visit across the Atlantic, but his affairs led to him in fact ending his days in the old country. Nevertheless, partly through Quaker diligence, his new town prospered, and through certain prominent individuals became the most important town at the time of the Revolution. It was also conveniently situated.

Rumblings over the desirability of independence began to take force in the seventeen-seventies with important meetings in 1774 and 1775 to which representatives came from the other continental states. Finally in 1776, after preparation by Thomas Jefferson, John Adams, Benjamin Franklin and others, the momentous Declaration of Independence was signed and presented to the people.

Among the signatories were two picked from each state, at least one of whom happened to be a descendant of a forebear who had found himself tapping the wrong shoulder at court! July 4th became the chosen date to celebrate as Independence Day. The activist Thomas Paine (1737-1809) was born in Britain but spent considerable stretches in America encouraging these people with his pamphlets and such works as *The Rights of Man*. He ended his days there.

The building where the actual signing of the Declaration took place is called Independence Hall, which can still be reached from Chestnut Street. It is claimed that the main chamber has not been altered in any way since that date. The Liberty Bell, in which Americans take such pride and which, when it was rung out confirming this historic moment, graced the top of the edifice, can now be seen close-to by tourists in its own precinct. Lo and behold, one is told that it was cast in ye olde England! Of course, at that period, many items and most which were manufactured came from the mother country.

Philadelphia became the natural capital from 1790 to 1800, and through the nineteenth century it continued to grow and to prosper. Grace Kelly (1928-82) was brought up here, surrounded by her sportive family, before becoming an actress and film-star, and then marrying Prince Rainer III of Monaco. Today the arts flourish in this cultural centre of long-standing reputation.

The capital of the state is now Harrisburg, a neat, becoming town which has had some German influence within it. State capitals are not necessarily the largest, best known or most important place, as in this instance. If you should enter the coach station, you might observe someone from the Amish Sect, an ancient community from Germany who continue to wear their distinctive dark brown garments with matching brimmed hat, and perhaps his young family along with him.

In the far west of the state is Pittsburgh. Some Clovis spears, the primeval type which is thought to have helped wipe out the mammoths, have been found in the locality which has led to the theory that they were brought across from south-west France, where similar specimens exist, during the ice age 17,000 years ago, the

Europeans eventually merging with the Asians. Moundsville, across the border in the narrow panhandle of West Virginia with its rural remnants, bears witness to the early presence of the 'red men', and its railway station, clearly added later, could still be labelled in the second half of the twentieth century 'cute' and reminiscent in cut and colour of the old Oxford railway station in England, whose country style became somewhat disparaged with the label 'temporary for fifty years'.

During colonial days the western region of Pennsylvania became heavily industrialized. Scattered factory chimneys used to dot the landscape up to the border fringed by the Ohio River. Particularly around Pittsburgh was the dark smoke noticeable, but no longer need an inhabitant born in the town, writing his life story, begin by pointing out that he first saw the light of day in manhood many years later on leaving it! Now the centre has been 'cleaned up', as the Americans like to say. It has been greatly smartened and modernized, thus earning it along the way the title 'capital of globilization'.

Washington, D.C.

The national capital was named after the General who became first President. He needed to be impartial head of all the states, so strips of land were taken from Virginia and Maryland to newly create what became known as the District of Columbia. The plot measured seventy square miles and contained a passage of the Potómac River. It might have appeared a bit swampy to begin with but much was made of it eventually.

There were thirteen states to start with and the number grew to forty-eight in the twentieth century. The expanse of continent was complete from ocean to ocean. Using D.C. facilitates the distinction between capital and the state of Washington in the far north-west of the country. 'From sea to shining sea' is the description of one sing-along anthem.

Additionally, in 1959, two further non-contiguous states were brought in to the union: Alaska, beyond the borders of Canada in the west, a territory which belonged to America since 1867 when is was purchased from Russia; and Hawaii, a group of islands two thousand miles out in the Pacific Ocean, where Americans had long been in control of the leading industries. On the 'Old Glory' flag there continued to be thirteen stripes but there were now fifty stars. All children are taught to pledge allegiance to this flag.

The map design for Washington, D.C., was originally created by a Frenchman, Pierre L'Enfant (1754-1825), and was based on a grid, as in New York City, but with diagonals as well. The first buildings were antique Grecian in conception with plenty of pillars, and their vast scale was relieved from being oppressive by their pale colouring. The essential element, the Capitol, with which Jefferson took some part in the final outcome, has a high, white marble dome, eventually becoming proudly familiar through photographs and giving momen-tum to Capitol Hill.

Understandably it took some time for the main public buildings to be completed. The second President, John Adams (1735-1826), from a Bostonian family, held office from 1797 to 1801, and it was Thomas Jefferson (1743-1826) who became the first President to live full-term in Washington, final capital city. Like George Washington he was from what was regarded as the Virginian aristocracy. He kept on his private home, Monticello, which he had built on a hilltop near Charlottesville. It is a delightful place, still containing many of his personally devised scientific creations. He has been credited with creating the first rocking-chair, a popular device in the States.

It was also not inappropriate that Jefferson should break fresh ground through residing in Washington, since he had been the chief author for the first draft of the founding documents. There have now been over two score Presidents of the United States, a goodly number. Jefferson did realize that all major problems had not been solved during his lifetime.

The Capitol remains the primary focus in Washington, being the seat of the national government, which is divided between the upper house of the Senate, constituted of two senators from each state, and the lower House of Representatives, drawn according to the distribution of population. Elections are fought above all between the two leading parties: the Republicans – emblem Elephant - who are to the right, and the Democrats – emblem Donkey - who are to the left but not as far as to be considered socialists. The native eagle is national symbol.

The west façade of the Capitol gives on to a stretch of grass. Gracing the north side of this are more government headquarters, including the National Archive where the 'top copy' of the American Constitution can be observed. With a few amendments, this document is held to have served the country well. No rush for you to discover the amendments and their numbers in which citizens can be pretty skilled!

Finally, within walking distance, one gets to the White House, beyond the green, with its own lawns and appealing style. Here the President resides with his family and here also much of government work takes place since the President is the most powerful person in the United States, and indeed, with some reservations, the world at the time of writing. The set-up and sequence may fundamentally continue, though cross¬currents inevitably bring fluidity, as with China.

The judiciary with the Supreme Court is also of vital importance since it is separate from the executive governing body. Other essential sections are the Treasury and the State Department, which is like the British Foreign Office.

One of the most striking edifices on the south side is the Smithsonian Institution, which in contrast has Italianate features and is constructed of red stone. Founded by an Englishman, it contains much scientific data with displays. There is a National Gallery of Art brimming with top-quality works and, of interest to many English scholars and actors, the Folger Shakespeare Library with theatre.

The principal diagonal route through the centre is Pennsylvania Avenue. Parallel to this runs Massachusetts Avenue which provides accommodation for a number of long-established embassies, including the British. From here ambassadors can nip across to the White House when required.

Georgetown, north-west of the central Mall, is a prized suburb in which to live since many desirable residences, architecturally superior, were built there during the first flush. On the northern fringe is Dunbarton Oaks, an eighteenth-century house with garden, now used as a conference centre. In 1944 a conciliatory meeting was held here leading to the founding of the United Nations. Igor Stravinsky (1882-1971), who became an American citizen, wrote a concerto honouring its name, which is regularly given an airing by the BBC.

Leaving Capitol Hill and turning south of all federal chambers and their fairways, one comes to parkland where the Potomac flows through grassy banks. Here, on the remaining north shore, are presidential monuments and war memorials. The most frequently reproduced in photographs, and therefore the one most instantly recognizable, is that with the large seated figure of President Lincoln.

South of the river, and so in Virginia, is Arlington National Cemetery which bears the eternal flame for President Kennedy. In addition, importantly, on this bank is the Pentagon, with an unusual five-sided conception, holding the Ministry of Defence and related matters.

Washington, D.C., is situated on what is regarded as the upper limit of 'The South', and as would be expected from this, it can often get very hot during the summer months. On the other hand, you can also get snow blizzards in the winter season. The ideal time to visit the capital is considered to be the spring when the cherry-trees are in blossom. This is a seductive moment for those who live in the catchment area.

John Philip Sousa (1854-1932), the composer of national band music, was born, appropriately enough, in Washington, D.C. He was the inspiration for both *Stars and Stripes for Ever* and *Washington Post*, surely the two most popular marches of all in the American repertoire. He believed no less in maintaining close ties with Britain.

Nashville

This lively town, founded in 1780 as an outpost, is the capital of the state of Tennessee. To the east are the Smoky Mountains leading to North Carolina, and to the north is Kentucky, gilded with Fort Knox and decked in blue grass denoting the race horses, but also a type of country music that was taken up in Nashville at the Grand Old Oprey, or more colloquially Ole Opry, the famous music venue that has been notably revitalized since the Second World War.

Before that time there was always a natural tradition of local talent which came over sometimes on the radio with such haunting favourites as *My Old Kentucky Home* by Stephen Foster (1826-64) and *The Way You Look Tonight* by Jerome Kern (1885-1945). If you should be missing your sibling background, *Home, Sweet Home* might touch you, another American number in verse, but with British composer, for sentimental category. Over in England, in some circles, American square dancing, with a caller, has hit a high. That is just one type of dance here among others to use up robust energy.

Nashville may be considered the capital of country-sourced music production now, but there is much more to the town than that. It is rich in Bibles and churches. From here the Bible Belt spreads through the mid-west, taking in Kansas. Nashville is rich as well in banking and commerce. On a hilltop is a striking replica, a precise copy, of the classical Greek Parthenon. Vanderbilt is the major university of the region with a central campus, and there is the prestigious college Ward Belmont for girls, with the capacity for concentration on music and dance. Tennessee Williams (1914-83) gives the latter a mention in his play '*Cat on a Hot Tin Roof*'.

A long morning's drive south-westward can bring you to the second town of Memphis, place of the birth of blues music and of the chosen home for the king of rock and roll, Elvis Presley (1935-77).

His colonial-style house Graceland is now a museum. There are many handsome, white-pillared mansions which can be seen in the towns and countryside of this southern state.

If you pass remote trees with old trunks, you may perceive bullet holes. These could have been made during the Civil War, for the ground was keenly fought over then. You might see a cardinal, a bright red crested bird. This is well down south, and the weather can get hot. The temperature at maximum will climb to over one hundred degrees centigrade. Mules sadly are in decline. Americans remain intrigued by their past, as any antique dealer will confirm.

A southern drawl may impinge on your consciousness, but if you have already dipped into Virginia the accent should not trouble you and becomes quite natural in this laid-back setting. You are probably also used to the profuse magnolias and dogwoods, long native plants to cherish. In hospitable welcome you could be offered a meal of fried chicken in batter with rice or red sweet-potatoes, that is to say yams, and aubergine, locally known as eggplant, or even beet greens, perhaps corn-on-the-cob to butter and salt an extra, all followed by a hot-fudge sundae which is also available in old-style drugstores and new-wave diners. You might develop a taste for genuine runny molasses.

There are good dentists in Nashville, for they are certainly not confined to Chicago or anywhere else. A young golfer from the town can find himself playing with success at the Masters in the parkland of Augusta, Georgia, where the expanse of America has been capitalized on admirably. Life, as far as Nashville, Tennessee, is concerned, has clearly moved beyond honky-tonk!

New Orleans

The French founded low-lying New Orleans, Louisiana, in 1718. Its position near the mouth of the mighty Mississippi River was seductive, even if the vast flow of water can cause problems to this day, as witnessed with devastating ocean storms in 2005. The Spaniards, who were immediately to the west, possessed the town for a number of years in the late eighteenth century until Napoleon (1769-1821) took it back again.

Everyone feared this man and there was at once a threat that the Americans would join with the English to throw him out of this vital, valuable river and sea port. Rather than be involved in fighting, Napoleon saw the opportunity to gain money and proceeded to cede and sell the area to the Americans, who in fact became the main beneficiaries.

Towards the end of 1803 the handover took place of what has become known as the Louisiana Purchase, giving America extensive land since the French territory stretched right up to the Canadian border. As the American flag was raised there was little applause, for the momentous event was no doubt unexpected for many pioneer families. New Orleans had become an original and rather enchanting place, with brick and stucco houses, many of them terraced as in France and backed by cyprus trees.

The centre for the export of cotton, rice and sugar, soon was receiving large quantities of wheat from the western plains. When steamboats arrived and the Southern Pacific Railway, the activity became even more dynamic with the contacts round the world. The town's population became more varied too, with all colours and all races. The products for trade brought refining and other off-shoot industries to this location.

There is an English-based community in the region as well. In 1815 'Stonewall' Jackson (1824-63) fought off a British attack, but the town fell early to Northerners, 1862, during the Civil War. Variety of background increased again, but the innate 'easy' culture, drawing primarily on African influences, began to make itself felt in the form of jazz and what became known in the twentieth century as traditional jazz. When you visit New Orleans you can stop in at Preservation Hall and hear some of the regional Dixieland Jazz. You could perhaps seek out a disc representing some of the former masters like Billie (the wife at the piano) and De De with his choice little band.

Nearby the Hall there are strip joints and local diversions readily available. The French Quarter is above all to be prized, and you can there partake of a continental breakfast or maybe just a French doughnut. Then you could take lunch in a restaurant with a patio courtyard. Carnival time before Lent is of course a highlight, climaxing in *Mardi Gras*.

Tulane University is in the vicinity and a wondrous weathered cemetery with massive ornate monuments to enterprising French settlers. An early form of the French language in the New World is still spoken in the area, known as creole, which can provide an interesting study in philology. Most people passing through may just want to view or ride in a paddle-steamer to savour past times. The mellow voice of Paul Robeson (1898-1976) and others, courtesy '*Show Boat*', reminds one that this river, slicing through America, is always there flowing along.

Nevertheless in the twenty-first century, apart from air-routes, there is the latest in bridges and highways, leaving literary lettered Mississippi on the eastern side, to bring you into town. Once there you might like to experience a 'superdome' enclosed stadium. The Roman Catholic cathedral setting, with a good old English name like Jackson Square, may bring you friendship among the artists if they are displaying.

Chicago

Multiple miles up north and a little east, to present a somewhat different scene, is Chicago, Illinois. Northerners are considered to have a lot of drive and it is here in abundance, using every sense of the word. The town was founded early in the nineteenth century and, once started, grew rapidly, particularly with the coming of the railroads, as the Americans call them. Both freight and passenger services became important to cover a western extension and sprawl. Then George Pullman (1831-1901) brought in the luxury coaches with sleeping facilities. In the first half of the eighteen-seventies Chicago saw two bad fires, but ultimately this enabled more substantial building. Chicago claimed the first skyscraper in the world and now has one of the tallest, Sears Tower.

Like in many cities of the United States, as elsewhere for air and prospects, industry tends to be to the east and the more appealing residential sections to the west. The not-forgotten architect, Frank Lloyd Wright (1869-1959), put up some family homes in the latter part of the town, namely Oak Park. The rigour of his style can still be observed in the present century, though such built-up boroughs suffer as elsewhere from modern pressures.

There is a rather delightful raised railway to bring people quickly down town to what became called 'the loop', because of its original circular motion in turning round. The centre of Chicago has much to satisfy needs: diverse shops to meet all tastes and latest trends, the Art Institute where you may gaze at the original of Renoir's 'Girl on a terrace', with many other impressionist paintings, the Millennium Park and elsewhere for concerts, and the Museum of Science and Industry containing an Apollo spacecraft.

Boosting the intellectual side, there is a premier university bearing the town's name with the name of Rockefeller occurring again as a founding benefactor. A full list of sports is pursued in Chicago, including basketball drawn from netball but with an indoor court, and horse-racing with two courses in the vicinity. The Kentucky Derby (pronounced 'er') remains the foremost race in the United States.

Due to its location nearly halfway across the country, Chicago has been a very popular venue for conferences. This all reflects in more restaurants — you could have a dinner at a Japanese one with your feet dangling below floor level, and there will be plentiful night-spots for clubbing if that is what you favour.

The region has acquired the notion of a culture of gun-slingers, because of the period in the nineteen-twenties when there was prohibition of alcohol and the so-named bootleggers brought drink surreptitiously across the border. Most notorious of the smugglers was Al Capone, with the result that the film industry has augmented the impression of a trigger-happy city. One must remember there have been many distinguished leaders and writers from the population, too long a list to mention here.

Chicago is called 'the windy city', partly for its 'windbags' holding forth loquaciously, but with major justification from the point of view of its position right beside Lake Michigan, the second of the Great Lakes. This water mass, which is 320 miles long, is sometimes known as the 'inland sea'. Winds can blow in suddenly and change the climate dramatically. At other times the prospect can woo ready middle-westerners, who like to come to the shore for recreation.

At one time Americans used to say if life got difficult, 'you can always move west', rather a better and different interpretation from 'going west'! That, these days, implies finished with completely. The west these days can still beckon. Not too far away is the state of South Dakota where, on Mount Rushmore can be contemplated the large sculpted heads of former Presidents: Washington, Jefferson, Lincoln and Theodore Roosevelt. This site could strike familiar from seeing it towards the end of the film, quite oft repeated, of 'North by Northwest', which first hit the screens in 1959 and stars English-born Cary Grant..

Denver

Denver, Colorado, is situated by the foothills of the Rocky Mountains, and its plateau has risen to one mile above sea level. For a day's outing you can easily rise to a thousand feet. The mountains, needless to say, are breathtaking and magnificent.

This uneven area was not quickly developed because of its nature. There had been an unidentified tribe on the site of Denver but had moved on without further known trace. Much later, in the sixteenth century, the Spaniards came, then in the eighteenth the French, but it was not until the arrival of the Americans that there was real development. The first routes west actually went south in the *Santa Fé* trail or north of Denver in the Oregon trail, their covered wagons etching history.

After the discovery of gold and then silver, things really took off in the eighteen-seventies and eighties. The remains of mines can still be seen on the hilltops, and grains of gold can be found quite readily in the streams with a little panning. A hundred years later oil was the draw.

The military now has a presence, and tourism has become a major industry with countless planes flying in and out daily. During the winter months skiing is a lasting draw. The smart set frequently head for Aspen, though there are in addition other captivating resorts. One could easily spend Bing's white Christmas here, warmed with a rum eggnog. In summer fishing is one popular sport, but all forms of relaxation are catered for in this line and in cultural pursuits.

The town itself is sought and admired. The civic buildings are generously laid out and older quarters lovingly preserved. The national mint is situated here too, producing nickels, dimes and quarters to jangle alongside your dollar bills! Dollars are essential to get very far, and 'making a fast buck' is what some characters are about.

If you stay in Denver any length of time, the open plains to the east will surely beckon. From Texas 'the Lone Star State' in the south to lush Montana in the north, this is cowboy country where cattle herds are driven and rounded up on ranches, while these days house guests are received for vacation. There are many tempting trails for horseback riding.

While you prepare for a wider tour, such names as Laramie and Cheyenne put you into a movie mood and excite your imagination with myths and legends of the wild west. To add to your recall of outlaws and heroes you may discover that Denver was at one stage the centre of activity for Wyatt Earp and his cronies who robbed a bank. You can view the original Wells Fargo building which is still standing there, besides a plush historic hotel. Buffs will be conscious most probably too that Buffalo Bill stalked his realm about here. A Red River sign may conjure up John Wayne for such enthusiasts before they get home. Rapid river rafting for the area can be sought as well.

As you head north you cover land which might appear monotonous, lacking wild buffalo, but in fact contained some of the final bones of the prehistoric life with dinosaurs. On your travels, livening things up, you could come across a native gathering or 'pow-wow' with Indian dancing and Cadillacs parked by the wigwams or, more prevalent contemporarily, tepees without the crossed poles. In a general way you may see airplanes garaged by the side of houses or parked in the front yard, as is the usual term rather than garden.

Reaching Wyoming there is Yellowstone to be experienced. The French traders were the first Europeans in the region. Then Lewis and Clark passed by as they made their epic journey which opened up the west to the American pioneer wagons. Yellowstone was the first National Park, started in 1872, taking you likely unaware it can be added, by an Englishman. There is much wildlife living naturally but under the control of rangers. Also here are spectacular geysers including such wonders as Old Faithful performing hourly to the admiring crowd and the vivid little Morning Glory pool bubbling gently not far away.

The park is on a longitude a small distance west of Denver. Coming down on the west side is Salt Lake City with the temple of the Mormons, the 'Church of Jesus Christ of Latter-day Saints'. The prophet Mormon was claimed in revelation by Joseph Smith (1805-44), hence the Book of Mormon. Brigham Young (1801-77) brought the followers out to Utah and their new home in 1847 because of persecution back east.

Thus America has its own Christian prophetic book. The community has proved successful and owns a famed genealogical table of family names. You could check your own out. These active people and their vigorous reputation rest on more than just a tabernacle choir, renowned though it is. The desert setting has seen miracles for them, and from central high ground the town, in its growth, has resembled Washington with its verdant tree-lined streets.

Wherever you go to mileage-wise, you are likely to notice the humble hamburger keeping going some bobbysoxer, old-timer or immigrant, whether with enthusiasm, poker face or necessity.

Las Vegas

Moving south-west through the state of Nevada one reaches Las Vegas, town of 'the wide plains'. Its dry weather has not stopped it growing amazingly in recent years, becoming an ultimate health spa, and altogether a must-see destination, with showmen and shopping juxtaposed.

It has had Mormons and Roman Catholics in its history, but it was the state's liberal tax laws, coupled with those for fast divorce close to get-rich-quick mining creases, that first drew attention to its advantages for people in certain human situations. Reno as well as Vegas was frequently sought for remarriage, but Las Vegas above all came to develop a name for its casinos and gambling rooms. Trippers stand today in wonderment at the number of individuals prepared to risk often large sums of money at the tables.

A new start in marriage is not forgotten either. In the fantasy world which no doubt exists there, a fresh beginning with marriage can equally fill with hope. Wedding signs to the chapels abound, making it all so easy, you could feel. Fabulous hotels, offering these facilities, and more, line The Strip, a roadway that needs no street lighting because of all the illuminations. Maybe you might join the avenue by Ceasar's Palace, just one of the infinite selection, it would appear, of luxury lodgings to patronize, with more restaurants than you can take in at once to sample.

These days the hotels are often themed which some experts think will become more common since `virtual reality' sites may be adopted as essential to avoid so many trampling feet on the originals. Americans have proved fond of Venice and now, among other reconstructed choices, you might stay at the Venetian Hotel. Contradicting this parched region of the United States, you can successfully take a canal outing in a gondola.

For more excitement there exist thrills among the heights, while for those desirous of something calmer and less demanding, a trip up an exterior glass elevator when dark can reveal an unforgettable neon transformation into the U.S. at night, shifting lights now spreading over the whole town. Within, on the lower levels, there will be singers and dancers, mainly from Hollywood, displaying their vibrancy and pace. When the chips are down, you may prefer a flash-in-the-pan experience and then to move along snappily, leaving behind the high rollers in glitzy Vegas!

Just south-east of the border, over in Arizona, is the greatest wonder in the northern hemisphere, probably both hemispheres, namely the Grand Canyon. Of all sights seen across the continent, this is the one above all that makes the most visitors, in recalling the event, take on a glazed, distant look in the eyes and speak with awe of what they have witnessed. Many people arrive from the opposite direction on route 66 to Flagstaff, but all end up on the rim of this incredible gorge, cut over millennia by the Colorado River. One may be gazing twenty-two miles across to the facing bank without comprehending the fact unless it is pointed out by a guide. Novices can just stand and admire the fantastic fixed view with beautiful multi-colouring, or descend past sheer rock formations in strata, covering a history of geological time, towards the valley floor fifteen thousand feet below. Alternatively, in a helicopter, one can get a conception revealing the scale of the canyon's range, which runs to a length of two hundred and seventeen miles (350km) with a width of four to eighteen miles (6-29km). The massive aspects are stunning, with or without new platforms.

If you are taken to the Indian watch tower, a performance may be scheduled for you. There are numerous native Americans in sandy, cacti-adorned Arizona. On one raised *mesa* (Spanish for `table') is the village of Walpai where the Hopi tribe has lived back to 1100, thus making this one of the oldest continuous settlements in the world. It is extraordinary how these descendants have survived in their desert, painted or no. The Navajo people have an extensive reservation not far away with more grassland. Some of these ancient native tribes show an earlier blood-group than the rest of us.

In contrast of style, the nineteenth-century London Bridge did not fall down, but was dismantled and reconstructed in this state of the Union over its vital river. If not a clash of cultures, a surprised raising of eyebrows might initially greet this information. The crossing has become an attraction in itself.

If you leave the Grand Canyon area late in the day, you may pass the Hoover Dam under its floodlighting, which is another majestic sight. The dam, over the Colorado River on the frontier between Nevada and Arizona, was started at the beginning of the thirties of the last century and named after its engineer President of the time. How valuable this resource of water is to the modern recipients cannot be exaggerated and is therefore worthy of this final comment.

San Francisco

Francis Drake in the *Golden Hind* is reputed to have stopped nearby in 1578 on his round-the-world trip. He would have spotted the bay which is the only natural harbour along the coast of California. The Spaniards were clearly the first Europeans to make a permanent impression on the area. The monks were around here by the seventeen-seventies, and a fortified settlement established and named in 1776. The Spanish presence was leaving its stamp on the whole region.

`Sierra' is their word for a range of mountains, and today we still refer to the Sierra Nevada which is crossed to move further west toward the Pacific and into the state of California. Its snowy heights and glacial depths resulted in the creation of the Yosemite National Park, one of the most scenic parks of America. On the slopes northwards are the grand sequoia trees, the tallest in the world, topping the Austrian pine. By them westward stand the related, also topping, Redwoods, making a forested fanfare above San Francisco. Their thick, red ridged trunks are a sight to remember.

Immediately east of San Francisco is the Sacramento Valley with a rich soil suitable for plant cultivation. The town of Sacramento is the capital of California, leaving the better known urban centres of the state to compete with each other if that is what they want to do.

In 1836 there was the agonizing taking of the Alamo, still standing in Texas. Yet ten years later, during persistent fighting with Mexico, San Francisco was annexed by the United States, whose own presence had recently become much more apparent in the area. Nevertheless, Latin-Americans have gone on arriving across the Rio Grande ever since, Latinoes.

The big boom-time came very soon after the U.S. acquisition with the discovery of gold in 'them there hills' just south-east of San Francisco. The year was 1848. By then the word could spread fast round the globe, and the immigrants seeking their fortune poured in from all directions, hopefully avoiding scorched Death Valley.

A terrible blow to the town was the earthquake of 1906, and there was a more minor one, too, in 1989. The instability of shifting tectonic plates in those parts is not forgotten, and allowance for vibration is attempted in any new architectural construction, with justification since there have been further rumbles through the state.

Inhabitants are justly proud of their handsome town. They like to think of it as built on seven hills as ancient Rome. People expect visitors from the old world to take a fancy to it, calling it the most European-like of American cities. The long-running cable car ascending the steepest central hill is indeed a fascination. Passing the small but chic boutiques and eating-houses on the way up, it is like experiencing a mini kaleidoscope with each moment to be savoured.

For many tourists the most memorable sight, and often the one they first see, is of the Golden Gate Bridge. This has a single span which reaches across the entrance to the bay. In some lights it appears really rosy and contrasts pleasantly with the blue of sea and sky. It was raised in 1937 and has become an essential ingredient of this tapestry scene. On the facing hills of the basin are Oakland and Berkeley (pronounced `er'), the latter having one of the most esteemed campuses of the University of California. Publishing, not surprisingly, is a major local industry. The whole bay area has many gracious homes, not infrequently with a view of the bridge.

The main part of San Francisco is on a peninsula to the south. By Fisherman's Wharf there are docked private boats of all sizes, and close at hand are plenty of restaurants where such treats as fresh oysters can be requested, quite strong drinks too if required.

The Chinese have taken full advantage of access to the bay, solely having the ocean to cross for a visit 'home'. San Francisco has had the largest Chinatown in the country. Their architecture reflects their innate original sense of style, with decorative lamp-posts and filigree endings to their turrets. Naturally there will be countless enticing, perhaps lantern-lit restaurants.

In stark contrast nearby can be seen the svelte lines of tall skyscrapers rising in the financial district with no salient features except possibly terminating triangular-fashion in a tapering point. Thus altogether there is an original skyline. Dipping away in a south-easterly direction from the town is the valley Santa Clara where electronic industries flourish, hence Silicon Valley.

Not to be forgotten and to add to this variety are the mission houses. You may catch sight of one somewhere in yellow stone with rambling wall vines. Welcoming above all to be visited is the pale-to-white toned Mission Deloris with its tallest section topped by a blending cupola and its interior offering a tranquil courtyard.

Therefore San Francisco combines a sophisticated life-style with a simpler ideology embracing flower-power. As you travel up and down and round about, taking in loftily modern churches and modestly trendy cafés or bars, you may find yourself solitary one minute and the next approached by an unknown, showing you all reputations of this metropolis still stand. Generally, the western side of the country is more relaxed and less crowded than the eastern side, with quicker access to rural reaches.

Maybe, although summertime, a wind is blowing through the gaps from the waterfront. This could be a sign for you to consider moving further south to a more certain barometer. There is an enchanting rail-route awaiting you frequently fringing the water's edge beyond the high cliff of Carmel. That is if you can find the departure point and not get swept into the Greyhound coach station and sorted through the doubtless milling population into the express service to L.A. Never mind, there will be from the window admirably cultivated grape-vines for you to inspect and not worthy of disdain. You are likely to find, if this happens, that you go at a good clip, though you may be unaware of the fact with the powerful engine.

Los Angeles

Once again the Spanish initiative in establishing the town is apparent with the name. Even greater has been the flux and flow of inhabitants to the region, and Los Angeles has now overtaken San Francisco in both geographical size and population. This, besides the all-round easier land access, is no doubt partly due also to the climate which is very appealing, the temperature normally stabilizing, even in winter, well above freezing point. Of course some would consider it too hot.

The semi-tropical heat range makes it possible to grow, with the aid of irrigation, a wide variety of fruit, including the citrus oranges and lemons, in addition to figs and grapes, not forgetting the raisins – fully sun-kissed! Not a few people speak of Los Angeles as possessing the worst expressions of Americanism, with what can appear never-ending freeways and shopping malls. Is not 'silicon valley' too, producing as it does every advance in micro-chip computing technology, taking over through skirting neighbourhoods now as it spreads about the state? To add to this situation, the saying is that what California does today, the rest of America does tomorrow. However, it can be pointed out that Los Angeles for long has had a flourishing Farmers Market, well before the English promotion of the term with turn-of-the-century fervour.

Any tourist coming to Los Angeles is full of anticipation for a sight of Hollywood whose compass and style continues to intrigue and grip generations. The year was 1911 that it began its growth as the world centre for film, though the frenzy of Oscar night was still some way off. Americans have always maintained their interest in the movies. The great stars of the mid-twentieth century, through their remoteness sustained by the studios, probably developed an aura not equalled since, but fascination remains acute for the novelty layer of each decade in the industry among the young. New stars ascend.

For those seeking some nostalgia there is on Hollywood Boulevard the Walk of Fame, the ground which bears imprints of former 'Greats'. Beverley Hills, adjacent, is where a number of the residential homes of former and present stars can be seen, but many of these idolized people now prefer to live much further away, perhaps Long Beach, for sailing, Palm Springs, favoured by golfers, or beyond. Nearer at hand is Santa Monica which is pleasant for an evening stroll. Maybe earlier in the day you have been able to visit a studio.

Universal has regular organized tours. Mainly, from choice, contemporary films are shot on location, but well known television sequences could frequently be in progress. Efforts are made these travelling days to see that visitors to Hollywood can have a good time in this palm-decked scenario. Rodéo Drive has become fashionable for shopping (note the 'e' of Rodeo has the emphasis in the Spanish way but, for the sport, Americans favour the first `o'). There is also Sunset Strip to be viewed. Facing the sea westwards, cliff tops can offer stunning sunsets.

Three hours' drive north is Santa Barbara, a calmer discerner's enclave. Here is the estate of the late Ronald Reagan (1911-2004). If many of his films were perhaps too unjustly disparaged as `B', he nevertheless became No.1 as President of the United States, from 1981 to 1989. He could be witty and speak with humour.

Taking advantage of the high ground in California near the coast, there are several astro-observatories, to keep the world abreast in other fields as well. Los Angeles, as would be expected, also has a top-class opera company and orchestra, flanked by a good drama department at its university, U.C.L.A.

There is the Hollywood Bowl as an all-embracing popular concert arena. 'Bowl' has topical usage. Its significance in the Rose Bowl pinpoints collegiate football competitions. It was the colleges that started the game of American football, for which the players wear helmets and padding, with use of an oval ball similar to that employed for English rugger. The Universities across America have teams able to compete keenly as soon as the autumn term, the first semester, begins. The Super Bowl has now been created, in which the major leagues perform. Female cheerleaders raise the tempo.

Baseball, the top national sport though already with 1755 reference in England, has long had the World Series matches. In addition to Yankees, there are names like Dodgers and White Sox. The game is quite a lot like rounders, but altogether tougher, and it is played on a diamond with four bases, the aim being above all to hit a 'home-run'. Babe Ruth, who died in 1948, has still not lost his hold as the most famous professional player.

East of Los Angeles, Walt started the first Disneyland. Besides all the iconic figures, the park has underwater surprises, surface adventures and land walk-ins which change frequently. The scope is always wide, covering mystery, exercise and education. It is a world apart, and yet close to hand in conception. Fun can be found for all ages.

Pasadena provides another artery to Los Angeles. Rather than any institute of technology it can make one call to mind the old-time 'Roof Orchestra', but there is more to the pleasing area for recreation than that. Not far away is the Huntingdon Library, located in sizeable grounds with a variety of stylized gardens such as the Japanese. In the accompanying gallery to the library is to be seen the unique collection of dominant paintings representing the nascent English school of the eighteenth century, with works by Gainsborough, Reynolds, Lawrence and others. It is a magnificent cache.

On a raised bank along the coast is the newer Getty Museum, built in the fashion of a Roman villa. This was founded in hideaway Malibu at the instigation of Paul Getty (1892-1972), the oil magnate who spent his final years in England. It is the highest-funded art gallery in the world and continues to draw in primary pictures, and other artwork.

Los Angeles has ample museums to draw attention to all levels of local civilization through the ages. To get about the place for most citizens, an automobile does become a necessity. For many, it can be necessary even just to get down the driveway! English people, at such a stage of voyaging, may feel they are missing a homely country cottage with a cup of tea. Looking round at the vegetation it is likely to be sub-tropical so that a glass of sugared ice-tea with lemon and a straw may be recognized as more appropriate.

If it is the cocktail hour and you were in New York, now over two thousand miles away, you might raise your glass with a 'Manhattan'. Remember that usually the strongest drinks display the fruit. For the southern heat you could ask someone to fix you a traditional long-glass 'highball' and settle yourself on a lounger to relax after probably a fair amount of walking. Often people just ask for `Whiskey sour' (note the common spelling with an 'e'). To carry your thoughts over 'the pond', now at least eight hours ahead, you could be offered Bourbon, even if Kentucky, or Scotch. Some Americans are drawn to Canadian rye which is less strong than the Scottish. You will not be out of place if you simply stick to fruit juice.

You must generally remember that individual States have many of their own laws and regulations so, by the time a news bulletin has dealt with national news too, there is less space for the international. This may leave a visitor a bit bereft and 'floating', a somewhat unusual experience.

Hopefully, if your mind is now turning to departure and you do not have a car, you will have booked any transport required. There are at least two airports able to take you out of town. Queues at the coach concourse on a busy morning in season have to be seen to be believed. If, *en route*, you descend from a vehicle ('coach' is the term preferred over 'bus), always note its number. Such are their dittoes in line to be reckoned with, you need to be sure you can find your way back quickly and correctly. A place to watch out about might be Phoenix for the docking of your 'ship of the desert', particularly in the middle of the night.

George Washington
1732 – 1799

The first President of the United States was born on 22 February 1732, in the county of Westmoreland, northern Virginia. When people among the royalist Cavaliers started arriving from England in the mid-seventeenth century, they tended to go to the state of Virginia, thereby manifoldly increasing the population in that region after a slow start, and balancing the population of the Puritans who went to New England.

So it was that George Washington's family left behind in England a small but charming estate, Sulgrave Manor in Northamptonshire which, as it happens, is also the county of the family of Diana Spencer who became the Princess of Wales, though Sulgrave is further south. The estate is now visited by many Americans. Forebears had previously retained their ancestral seat up in the town of Washington near beautiful Durham in the north.

A curiosity at Trinity College, Oxford, in the oldest part of the buildings, signalling former Durham College, is a small window until recently containing a crest of three stars and two stripes, said without doubt to be that of the Washington family. There is more than one theory about how the U.S. emblematic flag originated, as for instance with the stars of Amerigo Vespucci, but this later connection must clearly be a leading contender, and has been accepted for long as the primary source.

Augustine, George's father, was a planter on their lands in Virginia, and his mother, Mary Ball, was his father's second wife, George being the first issue of this union. The young George much admired the eldest of the children, his half-brother Lawrence, who was sent to

England for some education. On his return to America he married into the Fairfax family, who owned extensive land in Virginia.

As a result, George was sent down beyond the Blue Ridge Mountains, which beautifully perpetuate their name but are still part of the Appalachian range. George went to survey the territory westwards, and before long he became involved in the campaign 1753-57 against the French and American Indians. It has been said that George hoped for a promotion from the British army which he did not receive.

Be that as it may, in 1759 he made a successful marriage to Martha Dundridge Custis who was a widow of the same age and had several children whose descendents have come down to the present day. George took his bride to Mount Vernon, the family portion he had by then inherited from his half-brother Lawrence. It was a pleasant modest house which he enlarged.

Through his contacts with local government and trade he became aware of the fact that money through taxes was being sifted off to Britain. The standard of living generally was now rising faster in the States and the British may well have felt they wanted a share from their rich new lands. The long and the short of it was that after the Stamp Act was introduced, there was a fight for independence for which George Washington, who had gained some military experience, became Commander-in-Chief

With the fighting over, Washington returned to his estate. He was now the obvious choice as first President, and Mount Vernon being only fifteen miles from what was finally to be the capital, it was conveniently placed. His expertise in matters political may have been somewhat limited but he had become greatly revered.

Alexander Hamilton (1757-1804), who was born in the West Indies, had studied law in New York and assisted Washington in setting up a viable government. Due to his background, George was rather right-wing. Thomas Jefferson was by nature more to the left, and so already the two-party system was dawning to form a basis for government.

Washington was President from 1789 to 1797 and then returned to his home, Mount Vernon, with his wife. Both George and Martha were held in high affection and the new country, looking for an ideal to present to the young, found it in them. Mythic tales grew up about George as a boy; so, unable to tell a lie, he had confessed to his father of cutting down a cherry-tree. It is true that he was fond of trees and planted many, but actually surprisingly little is known about his childhood. This enables people willingly to follow their own fancies about this momentous and unprecedented step in history.

Abraham Lincoln
1809 – 1865

President Lincoln, already at number sixteen, was born on 12 February 1809, the son of Thomas Lincoln and Nancy Hanks Lincoln, who lived in the backwoods of Kentucky. Abraham therefore started his life in a log cabin for which he ultimately became nationally famous. 'From log cabin to White House' would be a slogan oft repeated to show that it was possible to reach the top position from humble origins, though it has now proved extremely difficult to be elected President without being a wealthy person, say a millionaire. Lincoln moved westwards with his father, a true frontiersman and farmer. They ended up in Illinois.

His mother, who had taught Abraham to read, died when he was only nine, and his father married again soon afterwards Mrs Sarah Bush Johnston whom he had admired as a youth. She helped Abraham to further his education, which was valuable because he was almost completely self-taught. He grew up a lanky but robust young man all of six foot, four inches, tall.

Finally he concentrated his studies on law, which is always useful for an aspirant interested in politics, and was accepted at the bar. He spent some time attached to a law firm in Springfield and served as a member of the state legislature from 1832 to 1842, the latter being the year Abraham married an attractive young girl, Mary Todd of Springfield. Both families had previously had a connection with Kentucky. The couple's eldest son was the only one to survive into adulthood.

In 1856 Lincoln joined the newly formed Republican Party. He had been demonstrating his fluency with words and, after a brief period in the senate, found himself elected President of the United States, which, with renewal in 1864, he held from 1861 to 1865.

On his election the Confederate southern states seceded from the other states. Subsequently Fort Sumter, the federal garrison in Charleston, South Carolina, refused to evacuate as requested to do. Lincoln was determined to preserve the Union. It was war, the Civil War. Ulysses Grant (1822-85) commanded the northern Yankees and Robert E. Lee (1807-70) led the Confederate armies. After the battle of Gettysburg proved a decisive victory for the north, Lincoln gave his much admired Gettysburg address reiterating the democratic principles of the Constitution. There was also the Emancipation Proclamation for the freedom of slaves.

Then, five days after Lee gave his formal surrender, John Wilkes Booth (1839-65), an actor, fatally shot President Lincoln at the intimate Ford's Theater in Washington on 14 April 1865. The Theater (note spelling) has been kept as a memorial to Lincoln, who did his best for reconciliation.

One of the less happy aspects of the aftermath was the arrival of imaginatively named `carpetbaggers' in the south. They had all their possessions, so the southerners said, in a carry-bag and came to make a notorious fast buck. Some of them were reported to have done so, and it was no doubt a difficult time for the losers. Some southerners will tell you the battle is still being fought!

Among Lincoln's last acts was to initiate the construction of the trans-continental railroad. It took six years to complete and would make an enormous difference to the trade figures and living conditions of the country, while backing up the saying, 'America never does anything by halves!' The line bore far-reaching consequences for the Indians too, who, not to be wondered at, loathed the iron horse. At first they had some success in resulting battles, such as Custer's 'last stand', but then lost out noticeably. They were courageous people who held on, and now again there are some who are quite wealthy and prosperous.

Principally it is the inspiring phrases of Abraham Lincoln given at the inauguration of the Gettysburg memorial ground which live on, extolling the vision 'that the government of the people, by the people, and for the people shall not perish from the earth'.

Theodore Roosevelt
1858 – 1919

Theodore Roosevelt, who spanned two centuries, has now faded into history, as is the fate of all politicians of the moment. He was born on 27 October 1858, and came from a successful Dutch family, whose first forebear in the United States arrived in 1749 as part of what was soon to become New York. His mother, Martha Bullock, had been brought up in the southern state of Georgia, where family members were prominent. As Theodore spent some time out west, where he had a ranch, he was a good representative for the whole country.

He had travelled abroad in his youth too, making a trip up the Nile. He attended Harvard and studied law at Columbia University. He proved a successful boxer, another sport esteemed in the U.S., since it has sometimes been particularly necessary there to be able to defend oneself. Theodore, during troubles, fought for a while in Latin America and was considered courageous. As he also wrote books, he could be called an all-rounder. *The Winning of the West* ran to four volumes.

He became Governor of New York in 1898 and soon found himself President of the United States between McKinley, for whom he was first Vice President, and Taft. At forty-two he was the youngest President so far, and numbered 26th in line, serving from 1901 to 1909. He always took an interest to the point of activity in international affairs, resulting in his award of the Nobel Peace Prize in 1906. Although he was a member of the Republican Party, which was to the right, his views did appear to shift towards the more liberal so that he was abandoning the more conservative element of the Party. He was even the first President to moot the idea of a national health service, for universal medical care.

He married twice, first Alice Hathaway and, after her death, Edith

Kermit. He had six children in all. Theodore had a sister in New England whom he liked to visit. He would always take every opportunity to go for long walks. It was early days for the motor car.

In fact he was an outdoor man who promoted national parks and liked to go big-game hunting. The famous occasion arrived when he refused to shoot a bear cub. The German firm Steiff was the first to make stuffed toy bears, but it was a New Yorker who initially suggested the designation 'teddy' after Theodore Roosevelt. The name was fortuitous and stuck. It was a little late, but a wonderful bit of unexpected publicity!

In addition, Teddy Roosevelt was the first to call his presidential mansion 'the White House'. This also struck a chord and stuck. The lightsome name has been admired and copied.

Franklin Delano Roosevelt
1882 — 1945

A while on into the twentieth century is another Roosevelt taking centre stage. Franklin was a distant cousin of Theodore, being the son of James. Both his parents were well-to-do, with a fine residence, Hyde Park, by the Hudson River in up-state New York. Franklin's mother, Sara Delano, was partly of French Huguenot extraction, since the surname was anciently de la Noye.

FDR, as he came to be known, was born on 30 January 1882, an only son. He received some of his education in Europe, which he visited frequently with his parents, and some at Groton, the smart American English-style private school. He then attended Harvard and Columbia, thus completing his legal studies.

So his life really developed in a very similar fashion to that of Theodore, if somewhat grander. After a period as a senator, followed by Governor of New York, 1929 to 1933, he was elected 32nd President of the United States. He had received useful experience of government under Woodrow Wilson (1856-1924) during the First World War which stood him in good stead.

In 1921 there was a difficult time for him when he contracted polio, but he did not let this fact deter him from pursuing a political career. Since it was an era before universal television and also a basically courteous age, he was able to use a wheelchair without it receiving undue prominence.

He had flair and confidence. The year 1929 saw the shattering Wall Street crash, followed by years of depression. Franklin is above all famous for taking full advantage of his presidency to introduce a 'New Deal' for workers which provided economic and social reform. He had to combat the Supreme Court to put through some of the progressive legislation, and there were elements, even in the Democratic Party, to which he belonged, often eager to restrain him. Nevertheless, the measures he initiated proved popular with the general public, and in 1936 Franklin was re-elected President with a resounding victory.

A quieter, subtle way in which Franklin Roosevelt influenced American life was by fixing more firmly the annual Thanksgiving Day, which is now celebrated regularly on a Thursday at the end of November. It was originally a form of Harvest Festival when goods were traded with the Indians. It has become the honoured time of year when families get together for a traditional reunion with a meal usually consisting of turkey followed by pumpkin pie. To an outsider it does in fact, through its uniqueness, appear to have established itself as an essential ingredient of 'the American dream', still a potent force in spite of periods of hardship and difficulty.

With the Second World War Franklin Roosevelt had to overcome a strong isolationist lobby. Again he succeeded in re-election, which was 1940. He started lend-lease to assist Britain by supplying weaponry and food. Occasionally he took to meeting Churchill secretly, perhaps in North America, perhaps in mid Atlantic. The Vultee-Vanguard P48 plane, a nippy item, was added in 1941, being christened for the first time ever with liquid oxygen. An outline for the Atlantic Charter was drawn up, for Roosevelt viewed conflict on a world scale. It was after events at Pearl Harbour in the Pacific, December 1941, that the United States joined the war and FDR began attending many conferences to plan for the peace, including trips to Casablanca on the Atlantic coast and Yalta in the Crimea. He could have been tougher with Stalin, but in wartime his stance was accepted.

Roosevelt was elected to a fourth term of office in 1944. As people said, he was definitely beginning to 'show his age'. Americans took to referring to this, but of course one had to remember that people from the opposite party could be as passionate for their side as enthusiasts in the U.K. It was, however, felt, after Roosevelt's death, that Presidents should only qualify for two terms of office, which is now legally binding. Elections for this post continue to be held early in November every four years.

To assist Franklin, he had his formidable wife, Eleanor (1884-1962). She was also a Roosevelt by birth and in fact more closely related to Theodore, being his niece. She and Franklin had six children. Eleanor was a tall, gracious lady, much admired for her humanitarian work. She showed interest in numerous social issues, such as minority groups, which have come to the forefront now. She was, in addition., a noted journalist in her own right.

After becoming a widow, Eleanor was made Chair of the U.N. Commission on Human Rights (1946-51), and such became her standing and promotion of female activity that one can be told, as a result, more is made of her since her passing for visitors to Hyde Park mansion than of Franklin. It should not be forgotten, though, that Franklin D. Roosevelt, through his forceful personality and humane vision, has been judged to rank by historians among 'the Greats'.

John Fitzgerald Kennedy
1917 – 1963

John F. Kennedy, or Jack as he used to be known, was born on 29 May 1917 of Irish parentage, and became the 35th President of the United States. His home town was Boston so, not surprisingly, he also attended Harvard University, leaving *cum laude,* but the two presidents immediately before him did not attend that University.

His father, Joseph Kennedy (1888-1969), was ambassador to Great Britain from 1937 to 1940, so Jack who spent time in England had experience abroad. He was part of a large family which would end up famous. Sadly the eldest son, Joe, on whom there were high hopes, died on a flight mission toward the end of the Second World War, so that an invisible mantle did at once fall on Jack because father, it was said, had political ambitions for his dynasty. There were younger brothers, Robert and Edward, who followed in a somewhat similar vein, and many sisters. Robert soon suffered the same fate as his elder brother and died early. Their mother, Rose Fitzgerald Kennedy, would live to a great age.

During World War II, Jack played his part by joining the Navy and was wounded heroically in the Pacific, afterwards famed for his rocking-chair. When peace came he entered Congress, first from 1946 in the House of Representatives, and then from 1952 as a member of the Senate. In 1953 he married Jacqueline Lee Bouvier (1929-94) who had been to all the right schools, including the prestigious Miss Porter's School in Farmington, Connecticut. His popular piece of writing, *Profiles in Courage* appeared in 1956.

Then at the end of the fifties, Kennedy threw his hat into the ring for the Presidency and was adopted as the Democratic candidate.

Some people said he looked too young. He was the youngest President on election day, but he also had quite a boyish look which emphasized the point. Others said he would fail because he was a Roman Catholic. None from that faith had been elected before, though that religious denomination is well represented in the population. He was standing against Richard Nixon (1913-94), and their appearance on television in debate was thought to favour Kennedy, confirming the continuing growth in importance of that medium.

Jack Kennedy was narrowly elected and, drawing on his erudition and travel, referred during his inaugural speech in January 1961 to the 'liberty' established in Magna Carta, of 1215. Later, he would impress Germans by stating '*Ich bin ein Berliner*'.

Meanwhile he was intriguing Americans with the family life-style. He brought new young intellectuals to Washington from the universities and invited a variety of famed individuals to the White House, including among them musicians to perform in concert. People were rather amazed to realize the First Lady was from the minority socialite group in this supposedly levelled-down society. She was definitely 'classy', as the Americans would say, and they read with fascination of her expensive shopping expeditions to Paris. Through confidence in her own taste, the mansion was redecorated. Altogether, it was 'Camelot'!

There were two small children, Caroline and John-John to complete the enchantment, occasionally even livening up the work-orientated Oval Office in the West Wing. Sometimes the family would go up to the Kennedy compound at Hyannisport on Cape Cod for a beach-side break. Private swimming pools were becoming quite common by now in America, so there was no need to feel overwhelmed by any luxury, but the public did not cease on the whole to be charmed by the pictures that were printed.

Jack had some big issues to face, though he had less than three years to show results. The Bay of Pigs' invasion of Cuba was a rather unfortunate episode he got himself involved with, but he redeemed his position in his firm stand against Russia's Kremlin, leading to the withdrawal of planned missiles on Cuba. There was success and failure. Third infant, Patrick, did not survive.

Then came the fateful state visit through Dallas, Texas. On the morning of 22 November 1963 JFK was being driven in a motorcade beside his wife when he was hit by a fatal bullet. This turned out to be caused by a deranged, so-called lone sniper, Lee Harvey Oswald (1939-63), who was in turn gunned down after being captured. The world was horror-stricken at these events, and the ensuing majestic, sad state funeral was universally watched through the power of television.

Jackie had to sustain herself and bring up her two children as best she could without the accustomed fatherly support. After a period of time she remarried, to the Greek shipping magnate Aristotle Onassis (1906-75), and was able to spend much of her life overseas with the children, mainly on a Greek island. Her final years were passed appropriately back in the United States.

Then son John, having grown to manhood, died tragically when flying his fiancé to the smart holiday island of Martha's Vineyard off the New England coast. Daughter Caroline was married and had children. Up to the new century she lived in comparative privacy among her own family, politics never far away.

Jack Kennedy had many facilities and national institutions renamed after him, including the main New York airport, often referred to now as `JFK'. He will not be forgotten. His charismatic brother Edward lived on until 2009, providing support for his relations and liberal contributions to his country and beyond.

William Jefferson Clinton
Born 1946

This President liked to be known as Bill. He was casual about it all, as such matters go, and some people were not keen on informality, thinking he should more frequently appear fully suited. It was all probably a sign of the times, but also it can be realized that he came up from a comparatively modest background.

Bill was born in the remote town of Hope, Arkansas, on 19 August 1946. His father, William Blythe III, died from a car accident before the boy was born. His mother, Virginia, left Bill with his grandparents, Hardie and Mattie Hawkins, while she completed her nurse's training. On her return she was then married again to Roger Clinton.

After various ups and downs the family in its new guise moved to Hot Springs, where Bill settled well in school. As a teenager he took his step-father's name of Clinton so as to feel properly part of the unit. Bill attended Georgetown University in Washington, D.C., and from there won a Rhodes Scholarship to Oxford University in England.

He was away in this capacity from 1968 to 1970. It must have been a mind-shaping experience for this southerner. Great interest has been shown in where he went and what he got up to while over in Europe. You might be able to say for starters that he avoided the draft for Vietnam, but he was away continuing his studies so who could blame him at that stage? He proved to have a natural facility as a writer and, on his return to the States, completed his education at Yale University Law School in 1973. While there in New Haven he met Hillary Rodham, from Chicago, whom he subsequently married.

In 1975 he became Attorney General of Arkansas, and then from 1979 to 1981, and from 1983 until his Presidency, he was Governor of Arkansas. He ran his campaign for the Democratic Party nomination and candidacy, with Al Gore as running mate for the Vice-Presidency.

Clinton at all stages was regarded as somewhat of an outsider, but at each hurdle he succeeded in rising to the occasion. Again there were television appearances, and here again he was able to confirm his capacity to appeal to the masses. He denied George Bush, Senior, a second term, but was followed by George W. Bush, his son, who is sometimes referred to as 'W'.

Bill never seemed able to avoid a certain amount of controversy, and this applied also to his years in office, 1993 to 2001. Former Presidents could really have been queried as well on many points, including the sexual, but these were more investigative days when everything was expected to be more open. There are always men and women round the President ready to take advantage of any opportunity for advancement, so all need to tread carefully!

Workwise, Bill Clinton was faced, like those in control of the White House before him, with pressing issues to ease and solve. There were deficits to cut in a general recession. Hillary was involved in politics herself and was disposed to introduce increased 'medicare', but the time was not right for major action, and her prospects were shelved until later. Bill was considered to have made some reasonable and wise decisions, through his advisers, for economic stability. There was, no less, much to be coped with abroad, and here his additional experience out of the country must have been beneficial. He had chances to observe different gun laws, which could influence attitudes on those questions.

It has to be said though, with regard to achievement, that he ended up with majorities for theopposition Republican Party in both houses of Congress, which must have slowed him. You can be surprised how little interest is shown in individual politicians, low down up to the top, particularly of course when the opposite party is supported.

Bill fully completed his term as 42nd President, overcoming legal problems. He did display his ability to persuade and survive. After leaving office, Bill was able to assist his wife in her election bid as senator for New York, which sent her on her way. He possessed talents that could be revealed at the ballot box.

Chelsea, their daughter, proved a great comfort and asset to her parents. Following other centres for her education, she attended Oxford University as a Rhodes Scholar like her father, and similarly joined University College. This brought Bill for visits to England, where he always appeared happy and well received. When Chelsea married in 2010 interest increased through him and Hillary too.

In 1994 he had been given an Honorary Degree by his ancient *Alma Mater*, which thus added a whole new dimension in the circumstances to the 'special relationship' between our two countries. Cecil Rhodes (1853-1902), through his widely spread scholarships, would certainly be gratified by the success of the bonding he envisaged and brought about in his own way. The English Speaking Union, among others, these days promotes friendly international relations, but Bill Clinton has his own niche as a pioneer in the regime of life. *Anno Domini* moved along for him as with all of us, however.

Still, while his wife with her forceful politics advanced as a female leader in the U.S., Bill, with his reputation to charm any company, moved to world prominence through his desire to improve his country's standing by personal contacts plus philanthropy. This was backed by his books, *My Life* and *Giving*.

Pocahontas
c. 1595 – 1617

Pocahontas was an 'Indian Princess', considered very beautiful and with this delightful name. The American so-called Indian tribes had much poetic language which has been preserved in the nomenclature of many towns and country-side features. The language could also be onomatopoeic, capturing the spirit of its subject described. Thus the state of Minnesota takes the name of a river running through it.

Pocahontas entered the early stages of Anglo-American history. John Smith (1580-1632) was one of the leaders of the first established English settlement on the continent, namely Jamestown of 1607. Situated some fifty miles below what eventually became Richmond, the capital of Virginia, it was a wild coastal area with Indians nearby, who understandably did not know what to make of these new arrivals, among them a few skilled Poles. There was a certain amount of hostage taking on both sides.

John Smith was soon captured and wrote years later in his autobiography how he was about to be felled with an axe by Pocahontas's father, a powerful chieftain, when his daughter, who was present, rose to Smith's defence and so, Smith claimed, saved his life. Later historians have often been prepared to doubt the veracity of this tale without any other supporting evidence, viewing John Smith as a natural romantic anyway. However, recent analysts see beyond moccasin make-believe and are more inclined to go along with the story, and why not? There is frequently more than a grain of truth in the world's legends.

Conversely, in more general friendly fashion, the Indians did help the colony through the first harsh winter. In spite of this, the enterprise did finally give out, attributed to a variety of reasons, but not for several years. There are remnants of the life-style still standing which maintain a notion of this seventeenth-century experience. In 1614 John Smith made an exploratory trip up to the area which, in six years' time, would receive the Pilgrim Fathers, not forgetting the Mothers! He was responsible for introducing the name 'New England' to what would become the north-east portion of the United States. Bartholomew Gosnold, newly hailed as the Founding Father of modern America, had himself explored the coast further north, naming Cape Cod and, after his daughter, Martha's Vineyard. He headed the first group to Jamestown, but only survived a few months and became unduly forgotten. Several important figures were involved in the foundation.

Eventually in this entwining test of human behaviour, Pocahontas, who had been taken hostage herself, converted to Christianity, being given the name Rebecca. The next year, 1614, she married John Rolfe and sailed for England. She was very well received there and presented at Court. For some while she lived in the region of Gravesend, Kent, and then, when in 1617 she was about to embark for a return journey to America, she died suddenly.

Distant contacts with New World natives have been conceived and crystallized in church windows and statuary, often without fully explaining why. Countless unidentified citizens, who eventually found themselves permanently in England, had shared for a period in the colonial patchwork. There are records of Gosnold's sister in the parish of Shelley, Suffolk.

Sometimes now in our adaptable world with much female emancipation, people will try to reinterpret, even more than they have done already, the partially known life of Pocahontas. Nevertheless, really most students who are introduced to this personality of enchantment, just want to preserve and relish the romantic image. A statue of charm has been raised in Jamestown.

Benjamin Franklin
1706 – 1790

Ben was born on 17 January 1706 in Boston, the eighth child of his father's second wife, Abiah Folger. He was the youngest son, and when his father who was a tallow chandler supplying candles and also soap died, Ben left school at age ten to help in the business. Soon, however, the boy joined an older half-brother who was running a printing and publishing firm. Ben proved talented and, wanting to be in charge of his own affairs without family constraint, exited for Philadelphia in 1723.

After a brief period in New York, it is said that he arrived in Pennsylvania only with what was in his pockets. A young girl, Deborah Read, joked with him about this. She took him home to her mother, who became his first landlady and Deborah ultimately married him.

Ben found a job with some printers and was soon again proving his worth. He was sent to England for some item in the works, and, once arrived, discovered he needed to take a local job in order to survive financially. This was just the first of several European trips, and he got to know Britain well, even visiting such English wonders as Stonehenge. He returned to Philadelphia in 1726 where they seemed to have rather forgotten about him. With his resourcefulness he found himself before long editing the *Pennsylvania Gazette*, and he started the 'Poor Richard' Almanacks, inventing a home-spun character to offer maxims and advice. This latter appeared successfully from 1732 to 1757. He began to make his presence really felt, and from 1751 to 1764 he was a member of the Pennsylvania Assembly.

Ben was sent to Britain a second time, on this occasion to negotiate the repeal of the Stamp Act on documents, with which he was successful, being a persuasive speaker, but he did not obtain all that he wished to do. He was something of a free-thinker himself, so all in all he was not satisfied, and thought independence with no strings attached was the only route. On his return to America he actively joined deliberations for independence and realized federation was needed for the separate states.

After complete separation from the mother country, Franklin was sent to France, the country that had sided with America, as ambassador where he remained from 1776 to 1785. He was one of the signatories to the peace treaty, and was well placed on the Continent, having taught himself French as well as Italian.

In addition to these accomplishments Franklin had by now made a name for himself as a premier scientist. Like many of the prominent early Americans he had developed an enquiring mind in matters scientific. He had invented a stove, produced the first bi-focal glasses, and, most impressive of all, introduced the initial lightning conductor. To begin with his ideas as to the electricity in lightning were treated with derision. When caught in a storm out on one of the primitive roadways of Pennsylvania, he noticed, arousing his interest, the behaviour of the climate close to the ground. He finally used a flying kite in a storm to prove that lightning is, as he had said, electricity, and at last the pure scientists had to take seriously his innovative rod. He had made a dynamic advancement in our understanding of primary forces.

Thus, in his life, he had become a respected publisher, politician, diplomat and, above all, scientist. He even demonstrated acute knowledge of musical instruments. The house in London where he mainly lived was, in the late twentieth century, made into a museum, and it is possible still today to find his bust for sale in English antique shops. Such was his fame when he died in April 1790 that his legacy has not been forgotten.

Mark Twain
1835 – 1910

Mark Twain is a pen-name meaning 'two fathoms deep', which Samuel Langhorne Clemens took from his experience as a steam-ship apprentice and then pilot on the Mississippi River. He was born on 30 November 1835, the son of a Virginian with frontier enthusiasm. His father had moved from Tennessee to Kentucky, where he married, and afterwards settled in Missouri, first in the town of Florida, the place of Twain's birth, and then Hannibal, right beside the river. That was where Samuel Clemens grew up.

Here was another whose father died while he was young, in fact in his twelfth year. As a result he had very little schooling, but this did not seem to matter! He acquired printing knowledge and, subsequent to helping his brother, Orion, on his newspaper, he took to travel going quite widely. After returning from his days with the steam-ship company, he went out west as far as San Francisco, where he worked with the contemporary western writer, Bret Harte.

He quickly became a success as a journalist and was soon sent overseas for the first time. He arrived in the Mediterranean area and visited the Holy Land. *The Innocents Abroad* resulted in 1869, and later he would write an original piece making an unusual stage production *'A Connecticut Yankee in King Arthur's Court'*. He could be ironical about 'Old World' Europe, revealing the essential being he was, a 'New World' frontiersman with egalitarian principles.

He was a boy during the great age of the paddle pushers and then, as a young man, achieved his primary aim to become a river-boat pilot for a large Mississippi company. However, with the coming of the Civil War there was a collapse in the service, and afterwards the railroads were taking over most of the business. Twain never forgot the golden age by the river, and this is what he brought to life so vividly in his famous novels, *The Adventures of Tom Sawyer*, which starts with the lad painting his Aunt Polly's fence, and *The Adventures of Huckleberry Finn*, the chronicle on and by the Mississippi of his pal in capering romps. The former appeared in 1876 and the latter was added in 1884. For them the author drew on all his contacts and observations among the varied racial groups passing through and settling by the river at that moment he was recalling.

There was humour and accuracy which was at once recognized. Mark Twain has been called by some academics the first truly American writer. *Life on The Mississippi,* drawing factually on his memories of this unique era, was also offered to much acclaim. Influences beyond the English are noticeable.

In 1870 Mark Twain had married Olivia Langdon who was actually from a conservative Protestant background, and they went to live in West Hartford, Connecticut, near the traditional literary scene. During a period he had Harriet Beecher Stowe (1811-96), who wrote *Uncle Tom's Cabin,* living in his garden house. He would have approved of her humanitarian sympathies.

For property he also had a rural retreat up in Vermont where he liked to go to do some of his writing. He had moved on from newspaper reporting to other composition and lecturing. Audiences enjoyed his often dropped anecdotal touches. He was involved, too, in a printing and publishing firm, where he had an unfortunate venture with a new typesetting machine which brought financial ruin.

Nevertheless, Twain survived and continued to travel widely, which gave him a firm international reputation. He had further hardships. His wife died before him in addition to two of his daughters, but you could say he was really wowed in 1987 when he visited England to receive an Honorary Degree from Oxford University. The twentieth century honoured him as he still walked the stage.

He could be satirical, even irreverent about European culture, but he was universally admired for his capture of the humorous turns of phrase evolving in American life, which manifoldly and evidently inspired him to both realism and imagination.

Many of his papers can be seen now at the University of Elmira in up-state New York. For a long time his house in Hartford has been a museum. An example of his numerous aphorisms, or maxims, with a continuous life-span is, on a too early press notice stating he had died: 'Reports of my death are greatly exaggerated.' You can see more in any *Dictionary of Quotations*.

Thomas Edison
1847 — 1931

Edison had a big effect on everybody's life through the coming of electric light. There were many other scientists in the field but he, largely through his dedication, got there first, or at any rate put discoveries to practical use.

Thomas Alva Edison was born on 11 February 1847 in the state of Ohio. He was of mixed Dutch and Scottish descent, and the family moved to the state of Michigan when he was seven years old. He was always interested in chemistry and the interrelationship of different branches of practical science.

He continued with his research and experiments even after going to work on the railways, which gave him the chance to travel extensively in the States and Canada. He became a telegraphic operator, and finally he settled in New Jersey, where he was from 1876 to 1887, in Newark to start with and then in Menlo Park.

He produced his most important inventions, including his electric light bulb, in 1879. However, for him there were many other discoveries already happening. 1877 witnessed the first recorded human voice. He made a successful photograph that year. An early cine-camera would come soon. Additional items he invented were lamps and batteries, also anticipating valves, and a record player.

Of great importance was his construction for a system of electric power distribution leading to the telephone transmitter. Then there was a carbon transmitter to create a microphone for the Bell telephone. Actually his first invention was an automatic repeater for telegraph messages, and finally he had over one thousand patents.

Above all, a dramatic event occurred in 1881-2 with the installation of the first lighting power plant in down-town New York for Wall Street. He had to persevere to get the balance right in order to prevent a fire breaking out accidentally. He managed this and soon other countries were developing the process, including France and Britain. Both countries, which were also well advanced in science, honoured this outstanding individual.

Among other competitive Americans was George Westinghouse (1846-1914). Edison started by promoting direct current transmission. A central European immigrant suggested to Westinghouse the alternating current system, which was thus evolved. Though Edison continued to support DC, AC did win out in the end, since it was eventually found to be more economical and more efficient.

Nevertheless, Con Edison became a vast firm across the continent offering a great deal of employment. Edison lived for over thirty years into the twentieth century and must have felt rewarded to see the fruits of his endeavours. A lot of power today comes from the area of Niagara and the Great Lakes.

Much of the gas lighting which preceded electricity was from wall fittings, and in America wall brackets are still quite popular. They can give subdued lighting and be smart. The devices may also give an old-world charm and, of course, Britain and elsewhere continue to use such systems through electric current. Electricity, and now with the sophistication of electronics, has become essential to modern-day living, being an integral part of lighting, heating and communication.

Thomas Edison at the right moment made a vital contribution. He even found time as well to write poetry. Looking ahead, he foresaw the coming of solar power.

Judy Garland
1922 - 1969

Judy's real name was Frances Gumm, but with her fame this was completely forgotten about, not surprisingly. However, she did have an early life with the name.

She was born on 10 June 1922 at Grand Rapids, Minnesota, the daughter of vaudeville performers. Her first appearance on stage was at the age of three. She then toured with her two sisters until 1937 when life began to take off for her in Hollywood.

Judy became a cute, young dark-haired performer with all the attributes: singing, dancing, acting. Soon she was taking part in musicals with Mickey Rooney for Metro-Goldwyn Mayer. The Hollywood musical was starting on its hey-day in glamour and romance, rolling off 'smash hits' as the saying goes.

Then Judy had the good fortune to win the prize role in her most famous movie of all, 'The Wizard of Oz', which appeared in 1939. This is based on the turn-of-the-century book by L. Frank Baum (1856-1919) about the child Dorothy, swept by a cyclone from her Kansas home for many adventures with her motley collection of companions and her dog Toto. Other versions can be done, but this is the one that remains popular and now in England has an annual showing on television.

Judy Garland was fortunate in securing a series of most essentially American roles. Musicals were clearly her *forte*. In 1944 burst on the scene 'Meet me in St Louis' (no 's' pronounced), where she is busy taking the trolley to the end of the line. It is a period piece with romantic razzmatazz, but preserving something of the quality of life in this fast-developing town which still liked to think it could compete with New York. The settlement early manifested its national style, and being in its position by the Mississippi River, became a gateway to the west. In the nineteen-sixties a state-of-the-art modern arch was erected to celebrate this. T. S. Eliot (1888-1965), the famed poet who came to England to live and gave the inspiration for the stage musical 'Cats', was born in the town.

The director of the last-named film was Vincent Minnelli who subsequently married Judy. They were the parents of Liza Minnelli, who had her own outstanding success with 'Cabaret', both on stage and screen. Liza became a close consolation to her mother in the difficult times ahead. But Judy had not finished with her great films yet.

'Easter Parade', with the dancing perfection of Fred Astaire for pairing, was heralded for 1948. Since then, has there been an Easter considered complete without it? The film certainly added kudos to the idea of parading in an Easter bonnet, or at any rate putting in an appearance to stroll in a town centre like New York. In that place there may be a few film stars about too, if you can recognize them!

As experienced by many stars who reach their peak, Judy was developing problems with drugs. In 1954, what was called a 'come-back' movie was released, 'A Star is Born'. This presented Judy in a more mature role, loosely based on Gerty Lawrence. It was Judy's film, though, and well received. Crowds flocked to the cinema and it kept her presence felt.

In her last years she liked to come to England and make concert appearances. 'Over the Rainbow' from her major success had become her theme song and was always offered with much poignancy. Nostalgia and affection abounded. For many there were war-time memories, and such events as her visits to England were fully reported in the newspapers. Judy actually died in London, in June 1969.

Her third marriage had produced another girl and a boy. In star style she had married five times. The second daughter Lorna, whose father was producer Sid Luft, has written a memoir covering her own life with her mother. She realizes that the icon Judy Garland has become does not diminish now in Hollywood or beyond. There is a new generation coming along. Soon, perhaps next Christmas, these young ones will witness for the first time a run of the classic movie none forget, 'The Wizard of Oz', and will thence be singing along, mentally if not out loud, with the eternally crowned characters as they 'follow the yellow brick road'.

Martin Luther King
1929 – 1968

Taking a bar stool out west a neighbour may offer the information gratuitously, 'I don't add up to much!' Martin Luther King always seemed to know where he was going.

He was born in Atlanta, Georgia, on 15 January 1929 to a Baptist minister, and attended Morehouse College there on a 'program for gifted students'. He then received a doctorate up at Boston University in 1954. Around America the doctoral thesis and award are very important. There are many professors and associate professors on campus, but to be a doctor through extra study is therefore generally considered to be more of a distinction. This notion and arrangement came originally from the universities in Germany above all. The German influence can be strong in the United States, particularly through the large number of settlers from that region of Europe who came to the mid-west in pioneering days. The importance of doctorates and additional studies could now be said to have increased in Britain under the closer American ties and connections.

While up in New England, King met Coretta Scot, a native of Alabama, who was studying music there. They were married in 1953. King's full name is Martin Luther King, Jr., for he bears the same name as his father. Thus they are Senior and Junior.

Afterwards Dr King became a Pastor in Montgomery, Alabama, subsequently returning to Atlanta. He was soon promoting in earnest his creed of non-violence to achieve his ends, which appears a reasonable thing to do, but he did sometimes get himself arrested. His efforts took off in the fifties and built up to a climax in the sixties when, with even closer communications across our planet, the plight of 'the black man' in the U.S., not forgetting the woman, entered ever sharper focus.

King became the recognized leader of the movement for change among African-Americans, as he sought to implement State and Federal civil rights laws to improve the lot of the disadvantaged. There were walks in Alabama. The crux of the early problems receiving world-wide coverage was connected with the schooling system. The most memorable moment came for many with the big rally of 1963 in Washington, D.C. aimed at the central issue, racial equality. Martin was a splendid and moving speaker. He drew the crowds.

`I have a dream ...' became his theme and catch-phrase, and well he might have one in this country which offered so much to so many. The W.A.S.P.S (white Anglo-Saxon Protestants) from the eastern coast had done a great deal in establishing a stable government, but the job was incomplete. Suddenly, taking longer than Rip van Winkle, America woke up. Billy Graham, in the nineteen-fifties, led Christian crusades to Britain, but King's influence, through technology, spread further. He had a wide remit.

In 1964 Martin Luther King received the Nobel peace prize. How ironic it is that this good man should be assassinated as he was in Memphis, Tennessee, four years later. Not all those in his racial group approved of his 'softly' approach. It is difficult for an outsider to understand such matters fully. There remains a certain mystery. He did become a martyr to his cause, and this prophet is much mourned. His wife has written her side of the story and 15 January is remembered in his honour each year.

America likes to think of itself still as 'God's own country'. The majority of citizens belong to some religious body, and nowhere else is there a higher percentage who attend church regularly. There has in recent times been an added freeing up and coming together. Much may appear contradictory, but there is that basic optimism which is sure to break through here in a land always proud to be thought new and modern.

A few years after King's death '*Jesus Christ Superstar*' was a hit with music and lyrics by two British writers, not American as one might have supposed. More entwined are the two countries than often realized. So for King times advanced.

Martin Luther King will be held as more than a civil rights campaigner who brought about integration. He is an important contributor to the national ideal who, in his complex journey, carved out his place in history. That meant on the international front too his haunting phrases were becoming firmly fixed and remembered.

Many people came to believe, with the election of Barack Obama as President of the United States, that King's dream had been realized. Obama had a white American mother but a black father from Kenya, a country of the British-linked Commonwealth one can point out, endowing him with the English language, and in addition incidentally that Obama shares a date of birth with the beloved late Queen Mother, 4 August, though in his case the year 1961 is much more recent. Although youthful to take office he does, with his background, potentially bring good credentials as a world leader. Martin Luther King clearly helped to make this important development possible.

Canadian Hi

The British plane was touching down in Vancouver, and there was at least one person on board for whom the landscape was a completely novel experience.

My name is Joan like my paternal grandmother who started our family love-affair with Canada, this delightful realm with lofty pines, sparkling water, and so much more. Yes, much else. My gran made her own visit as a child with her godmother, who was a Canadian with roots in the Rockies. Many had been the tales I grew up hearing, being told first and foremost of the great trip on the Canadian Pacific Railway.

Gran had arrived by steamer on river route to Montreal. The town, already with its twin cultures, had a certain sophistication, even though it was in the days before multi-level developments. This was the 'new world' but with a long enough history to embrace magnificent monuments to the past.

Mounting on the train here, Gran travelled for three days and three nights, just making a brief stop in the prairie town of Winnipeg where, so she loved to recount to me, she saw horses in straw hats! Reaching the mountains an observation car was added with a small outside platform at the rear. That was when Gran lost her own pretty straw bonnet with pink ribbons. Perhaps one of the population, who used to appear sometimes by the line from the trees to wave and smile at the receding passengers, found this gem. Following Gran's advice I have always tied my bows tightly! Simultaneous to the rise in ground, the bends became more pronounced, and if one struck the right moment, one could then observe two engines puffing at the front.

Yes, I had heard all about the romance of that trip, from feeding the chipmunks cake in Jasper National Park to standing suddenly on the shore of Lake Louise where the vivid blue reflected from the sky was deep and rich, somehow not the turquoise tone, pretty too, you are likely to see today. Linking with the past, Canadians do not want to lose the original haunting melody of their trains. The particular timbre of their bells can also be arresting.

My parents had later continued the saga. My mother's name is Emma. It was the generation of my grandmothers which had brought such favourites from early Georgian and Victorian times back into fashion. My father, a political scientist, was John after his father. Before I was born they had spent a year at the University of Winnipeg, so we were firmly bonded to the dominion.

Now I was coming to start my tour of Canada with their hosts, David and Ruth who, like many compatriots, had retired to the west coast where the climate was temperate and somewhat rainy, not unlike England. What is more, relatives from the last named in abundance keep in touch with residents.

*   *   *

I duly arrived via the international airport. Altogether unexpectedly I was told the Duke of Westminster owns a considerable amount of the property in residential West Vancouver, which rises on the hillside above the harbours and port of the bay. David had inherited his brick house through his family, which was from British Columbia and had worked closely with the native communities for generations. I was gracefully received by David and Ruth who took me to see the local sights. Shops displayed much green jade, reasonably priced jewellery in jade.

Ruth's childhood had been spent in Nova Scotia, one of the maritime provinces back east by the Atlantic, where she had delighted in the fresh clean air round where she lived. We were soon going out further to see more of British Columbia. We even went down to Washington State for a taste of the U.S., not quite as far as the finger lakes of Seattle, but far enough to get the feel of 'another place'. I bought a light, organdie dress as a souvenir.

By boat we went across to Vancouver Island where the University of British Columbia is situated. On the way we saw in the distance the black backs of many whales, soaring and sinking in the water. There have been natives and a variety of groups in the history of the island. Remnants of missionary activity and trading posts remain. Modernity gave me a fizzy orange drink.

Generally in the province, the number of immigrants coming in from Asia greatly increased at the end of the twentieth century with the change of status in Hong Kong. We liked to buy the fruit and veg some of these people had taken to selling on counters by the roadside. We used to take choice items home and Ruth would make a delicious fresh meal with young lettuce leaves, perhaps a banana, and topped with salad cream – a kind of Florida salad. It reminded me of the crops, including potatoes, both my grandfathers used to grow. At night we ate before a magnificent, illuminated panoramic view of the waterfront, which became riveting when a liner came in decked with fairy lights. Often houses in Canada are basement 'split level', giving aspects.

Most of all, maybe, I enjoyed our outing in a motorhome up to Prince George, which nestles deep in the Rockies and therefore is part of the heartland of the province. Here many of the old Canadian families have settled where can be lived a very traditional form of national life with, in the winter time, plenty of hockey, in other words ice hockey, skiing and skating. I was there in the summer, so we would stop near a motel with an outdoor swimming-pool for a dip, often having the water all to ourselves. Not far away were hot springs to be sampled as well.

Near these in an outside area was a cute orange bear who just stood and stared back at one. 'Do not think you can pat him', one was warned. My Gran told me of all the wild life she had experienced. There was the moose clambering down a steep slope and crossing the road as one came round a bend, two graceful deer suddenly running by the car, and the porcupine observing the scene from the comfort of a grassy bank. We ourselves did well too, with the increase of buffalo, or bison as they are called there, and numerous elk.

David was quick to spot any wild life *en route*. There were the Rocky Mountain goats, well camouflaged in grey, shaggy coats. Occasionally David would see animals by, or was it in, the rock face which no one else could see. 'You have to be born in British Columbia to see that one', he laughed.

Visitors are told these days to beware all bears. Particularly, if one is eating *en plain air,* they may smell the food. Soon, *à propos* this subject (to make some use of Canada's dual language), David was singing along with the song of Jonah being saved from the whale, Daniel from the lion's den, and then .... In full throat he took off with 'Oh Lord, if you can't help me, for goodness sake don't help that bear!' Red-jacketed Mounties to the rescue?

After a while, alerting for me, some brilliant colours were visible high among the dark green conifers. It was an array of totem poles, rising in their carved glory, and with wings to the side giving them full native symbolism. Examples can be seen too in the parkland of Vancouver.

With my compelling present being so full of interest, I had to remind myself that I would soon be leaving. So many tourists I had spoken to were heading for Prince Rupert, further north on the coast, with the aim of taking a boat up to Alaska. The Eskimos living there were now American citizens. In Vancouver museums can also be seen relics from polar exploration to remind one that the cove here had been a starting-off point.

For myself, David and Ruth were inviting me to stay at Crescent Beach, not far from their home, where relations had a tranquil summer place. At the bottom of the garden was an archway leading straight onto the sand and with the water close by of the Pacific sound. The summer weather there is warm and welcoming, mentally far from the snow-capped mountains. So I was able to spend a few last days relaxing in this retreat.

I had decided to take the coach for my journey eastwards. I could thus take a full measure of distances in this vast country, one of the largest in the world. We started by travelling near the Fraser River, and when I spotted the Salmon Arms down on the shore-line, I was taken back to my geography classes when we had learnt about the plentiful fish stocks. Salmon reach Scotland but here was superabundance. Canada is a land of enormous resources, above and below ground, and after inevitably taking a few extra bends and stretches than anticipated, we were over the border in Alberta.

During the twentieth century large quantities of oil were located and raised here, providing Edmonton with a multitude of glass skyscrapers. However, I was not deviating further north on this trip, since I had enough space to cover already! Leaving aside those temples to success with their swinging window-cleaners, hopefully from head-for-heights tribes, I made for Calgary, another exciting stopping place. This was the month of July and the Stampede was soon to begin. Calgary possesses the longest-running continuous annual rodeo anywhere. The numerous motels were filling up now. American cowboys were arriving to show off their skills. It was fun to share the thrill of the hour. Here and there brimmed stetsons were tilted over brows, lasso ropes slung over arms.

Passing along the highway again, I noticed on a signpost the name Medicine Hat. What history and enchantment of the west was up here in Canada too. Prominent toll-collectors do not appear as down in the States, present since olden days of raising the camber. Our route was now clear.

Eventually our wheels were turning through Saskatchewan and its capital Regina. For I was heading yet further east to Manitoba, where eternal values are expressed in this Indian name, sometimes as 'the wind of the spirit' or even 'the voice of God'. There are indeed many churches in Manitoba and variations within them.

For some time I had been advancing through an agricultural expanse which increased as it lowered and levelled. Thus I duly reached the most widely-known prairie province, its rural communities scattered with their raised, often shining water-towers. As

we approached Winnipeg, there was occasionally agricultural equip-
ment in cheerful colours by the roadside, reminding one of the basic
rooted industry, even of this capital town.

I was met in the centre by Michael, the son of my former hosts, and
he drove me to his home in the residential suburbs, where his wife
Linda awaited me. The children had gone up to bed, and the
downstairs had been lit with glowing candles in my honour. I had
never before seen so many of those wax sticks all together. The sight
was intimate and spectacular.

The next morning I met the two young ones, Peter who was seven,
and Amanda who was four. Michael worked for one of the
agricultural firms, so was often away for much of the day. Linda had
out on a ledge a sewing machine with which she was involved in
making a cotton dress for Amanda. Peter had just had a birthday, and
was showing off his new wagon.

We went for a walk along the neighbourhood pavement, or
sidewalk as North Americans say. It contained old-fashioned slabs,
which raised banter about Christopher Robin. The children did not
mind stepping on the lines, but tried to avoid the tips of their toes
touching them! There were some gradients for Peter, usually with
Amanda, on his wagon. Linda always made sure the children were
on the area of the pavement that faced the on-coming traffic, though
by mid-morning there was very little, and few pedestrians either.

Back from our jaunt Linda made some peanut-butter cookies and
set the wash going after brushing out any pockets. She did it all with
such ease that one felt she had picked up the local wifely virtues :
Kirche, Kochen, Kinder. Linda did have as well a part-time job in a
dental surgery, and there again, with thoughtfulness, she was training
her children to floss their teeth at night-time, counting as they went
along to be sure not to miss any.

With advice, I frequently took myself out to explore the town. It
seemed to me the business, university and travel arteries were not far
apart. One could mingle among them as they converged around old
Portage Avenue. I noticed large war memorials on a main thorough-

fare. The staples of life were all prominent. The local population had proved most loyal to the old country, linked in one world, and always, in the contemporary scene, gave visiting royalty a warm welcome, even when the climate, as in the winter-time, was definitely cold. At such phases in the calendar, it was not difficult in the vicinity to get snowed in for considerable periods. Such tales were part of the romance!

I was, on my own visit, naturally anticipating a glance at the university, but a little confused between the University of Winnipeg and the University of Manitoba. I am sure my father understood it all because he was regularly sent the literature about new buildings, which formed valuable additions, and former students, active in many fields. I enjoyed taking in a central art gallery, too, which possessed pictures of originality by artists with resident patrimony.

Recently tourists had become very keen on penetrating the northern wilderness, even going up as far as the polar bears out of hibernation. The caribou, North American reindeer, migrate. I ad-vanced to a certain degree and welcomed the sensation of remoteness among the more isolated Canadian inhabitants. To complete my sojourn I took a boat-tour on the extensive Lake Winnipeg. On this escapade, there was no notion of paddling my own canoe! In case I felt like putting my feet up on a deck sunbed, I took along a collection of short stories by the author who was the pride of the locality, Stephen Leacock. His humorous, untaxing efforts first hit the bookstalls in the early twentieth century, I knew, but are still republished and enjoyed world-wide.

When I got back to the house, Michael was tuned in to the final stages of the Calgary Stampede. Hanging on to cattle by their horns to stay aloft, or holding to the saddle on a bucking bronco, there were endless feats of daring to grip one. The top stars were getting interviews, but what fascinated me as much as anything was the tone of the jargon continuously used. The ethos is just unique, and not like that employed for any pursuit in England.

*   *   *

Once more, with plenty for rumination, I took up my journey towards the east coast. I crossed the border into the province of Ontario, and then headed southwards to the lake of similar name. On the north shore I reached Toronto. Not very long ago an easterner had said to me that nothing happened west of Ontario. Surely he was joking. I could not tell! Life is certainly changing with the tick of clocks, and I had already seen so much, up-to-date and hallowed with age.

For my approaching stay I had received a kind invitation from a family whom my parents had got to know through a contact. George and Anna met me and took me to their present home which was situated in the outskirts of the town. Formerly they had lived in an area close to where some of Helen Keller's people lived, that courageous person who had lost her sight and hearing as an infant, and yet grown up in the States to achieve a great deal for which she became nationally famous. My new hosts had moved when their two children were small. They were now teenagers.

Rachel had said she wanted to be a model. There was a becoming picture of her in the main room. She was slim enough that a two-dimensional photograph would not give her too much weight, and her moistened lips gave a shine. She was no more than fourteen when it was taken. Since then her singing voice had continued to develop, and she was shortly going off to Italy while considering whether to have it trained. She looked forward to finishing grade school when Valentine would be more meaningful.

She and her brother had been two attractive *bambini*. Colin was now himself fourteen. He had recently been up to Ottawa, the national capital, and was speaking of wanting to join the foreign service. He had brought back for me a souvenir, which was an artistic little bowl with a design etched on the dark surface. It had been made by the Inuits, who were a tribal people like the Eskimos of the U.S. in Alaska. I told Colin that I had heard it said Canadian diplomats had the reputation of keeping together. He would be able to test how much they did stick to one another! I thought this quality would be rather appealing, showing they were contented in each other's company. Canadians did have much to be proud of, not least being the country reputed to have the lowest crime rate.

George had been in the army. He thought the new national flag was more suitable for a garage depot. He was being serious since he could appreciate the symbolism of the old one, but times were required to move on for the next generation. Colin, like his father before him, was arranging to visit England where, as Nancy Mitford tells us, Canadians are readily accepted in society.

Anna had been brought up in a medical environment. Her father had attended McGill University in Montreal, a very prestigious institution ranking high beside all academies. She herself had spent a year down in the States, her auburn hair much admired, and had picked up the popular habit there of having a toasted 'English muffin' for breakfast with butter and grape jelly. She was not of an age to slip into brunch! The Americans got ahead with the delicacy of old-fashioned muffins because they invented the first machines capable of the technique.

Later in the day we sometimes went out into the countryside to rural settlements with old-world names for a cup of tea or coffee and a sandwich. It could feel rather like being in a cosy museum with items for sale, including freshly completed paintings on the walls. Then, one day, Anna herself made an angel cake, which was completely white with whipped egg-white in the icing, the opposite of a chocolate devil's food cake.

I naturally investigated in more detail the town itself. There was another university with gracious buildings to be seen, and the City Hall with striking rotunda surrounded by civic offices constructed in two curves, 'the eye of the city'. This was just part of the down-town development which, for a period at any rate, could show the highest free-standing structure in the world. Someone in a café asked me if I was an actress! I believe she heard my English accent and thought perhaps I was attached to their nearby Shakespeare company of some standing.

Lake Ontario may be the smallest of the Great Lakes but the banks enhance a plethora of towns and villages along its north shore. In one place it was pointed out where the Prince of Wales had danced. Never mind that nobody could remember which Prince of Wales. Edward VIII? The memory lingered anyway.

I could not fail to make a quick dart down to the junction where Lake Eyrie joins Lake Ontario between the United States and Canada to witness the mighty spectacle of Niagara. It gives a measure of the size of these lakes as the unfailing water cascades over the Falls, impressive from whatever angle. I noticed nearby a beaver family with many busy in their favoured occupation of dam building. The liquid would never run out for them here!

Above Toronto are many more lakes, and these are frequently favoured for weekend hide-aways. George and Anna had a cottage among the ubiquitous pines, never far away except in the flatter areas of the prairie provinces with their wheat fields and open spaces. By the sides of the lakes back east, countless loons , ducks and drakes call to one another, and their forms are artistically reproduced for tourist tea-towels, bottle-stoppers, etcetera. We took a break up at the holiday spot. I did not learn to water-ski, nor had I sailed or rafted further west. Some things had to wait, maybe to draw one back again.

*   *   *

The moment came for me to head for my ultimate destination. I was given an impeccable spray of flowers with orchid to wear, perhaps another idea from the States where the people admire corsages, and orchids supremely. Occasionally, covering such distances, I made a stop-over, but I also liked staying on the coach to cut the hours spent moving. Slacks and shorts were prevalent in leisure areas, the former particularly for travelling, but anything goes these days. Toronto has the largest traffic complex in the world.

Quebec province offered some rugged scenery with varied vegetation, and there were valued resources underneath, including oil. It was beautiful and bountiful, with now too an historic background. I reached Quebec City, where a family of French descent had offered me hospitality. Gilbert and Yvonne had one boy, Roger, who was ten. They lived in the old part of the town, which was on both the Upper and Lower Levels, the latter containing also the modern section where situation enabled it to stretch away into the distance.

French Canadians, inevitably, remember their history. Some, not surprisingly after bitter fighting in the Seven Years War 1756-63, think they were badly treated by the British. For instance, the schools had been interfered with, I was told somewhere. George in Toronto, on the other hand, thought the British had been too lenient which led to trouble later. At the same time, French Canadians felt let down by their home country in that reinforcements did not arrive soon enough to prevent their failure at the critical assault. There were many heroic and fine Frenchmen in the early pioneering days as well as Englishmen, and they are all recognized and respected today.

The numerous races of the New World have welded together a fresh culture with its own linguistic styles and accents. Old France likes to exalt in its own inherited qualities. Canada, today, is a strong country and most hope it can continue to keep together. As for England and France, they sensibly introduced the *entente cordiale* early in the twentieth century, encouraged by Edward VII.

Soon after my arrival in Quebec, a friend of mine from France happened to be passing through the area. I was interested to see, when we visited restaurants, how delighted management and diners were to talk with her. This individual form of bonding came readily to the fore. An afternoon before she left we toured together the picturesque Ile d'Orleans, one of the 'thousand islands'. We took a cab, and in a turning on this rural ride the wheels got stuck in a ditch. Our driver was fully resourceful. He found a large twig, placed it in front of the most offending corner, and we were off again.

At night the high lines of the capital were lit up, like those of the Château Frontenac, to capture the eye. One of the main definite draws for me was to go in the daylight, not long after my orientation, to the stretch of grass in the upper town above the Heights of Abraham. As I stood in the morning sunlight, somewhat surprisingly alone with no crowds, the stillness of it made one feel it was hard to realize the Heights had been scaled and that there had been fighting here. I stood for a while in contemplation on this spot, and then I moved round to the left until I was on the end promontory, looking right down on a section of the St Lawrence River which divided either side of me.

The long, smooth, wide expanse before me was a wonder to behold. I continued to be the only person there, which on reflection is amazing considering the number of tourists always about in these flexible times. A thunder-storm had preceded my arrival, and this appeared to have cleared the air miraculously. The scene was utterly idyllic. One did not notice any movement at all. Even the small barque, way below on the blue surface of the water, looked as though it was transfixed and had to linger too. I cannot think of anywhere else in whatever setting to give a finer aspect. The smart, attractive hotel, behind where I now was, did not tempt me inside. One had to savour the moment.

I could speak French and my hosts could speak English, so we got along splendidly. I was taken one evening to a new play which had been written by a French Canadian boy who was, in term-time, a student at the University of Quebec. There was quite a lot to grapple with in it, and my situation put me in mind of an intellectual Parisian lady who told me firmly, 'You should always buy a programme!' She was right too, if proper comprehension was to follow.

After the show I helped to take the family pet, a spaniel, for its last constitutional walk. This also made me think of Paris where, one night when out about ten o'clock, dogs on leads emerged from many doorways. *L'heure des chiens,* I was informed. Various nationalities display their affection for dogs in their own way, even if the English have the reputation for being the most sentimental. Canadians do not like to be too soft.

Roger was very fond of their dog, whom he called *Charme*. He often went to parks with his four-legged friend and, being a spaniel, the animal was instinctively ready to get to the water and chase the ducks.

In the winter months Roger would go after him even onto the ice. I told him to be careful when the ice began to melt. A Dutch lady had given me a warning when I was a child which I had never forgotten. If you fall through, you must always remember to put an arm up so that you do not get swept under what remains. Gilbert thought that was sound advice.

He was a business man who ran a multi-purpose store. Roger had not yet made up his mind what he planned to do when he grew up, and Yvonne was not for pressing him unduly about this. Whether he would follow his father or not was for the future which would have its own new structures.

All too fast for me the date arrived for good-byes, *adieux*. 'Time and the hour waiteth for no man..' Newfoundland is an island which has become a popular destination for some Canadians, being renowned for more than a dog. It does, however, require an extra hop and that, for my part, will have to wait. Labrador no less!

The next thing I knew I was in an eastern airport heading for home, my winged chariot before me. There were scores of people about who were just arriving, and not a few with a vast trunk or suitcase which seemed to speak of immigration 'with all one's earthly goods and worldly possessions'. For me, my trip had been a start to build on later.

I thought of this country, like the rest of us, moving continuously into a new age. Canada has been praised as being the only nation never to have fought a civil war. It is an admirable land, in its own way, from coast to coast. As we rose in the air I truly prayed that Canada would succeed in working out any further difficulties as they had in the past, together and 'OK'.

Quick Quiz

(Answers following overleaf)

1. The largest whale in the world may be swimming about the Pacific Ocean, one hundred feet in length (thirty metres), but is nevertheless reported to be difficult to find. Which one is this?

2. The oldest known religion in the world believes in reincarnation. Can you name it?

3. The founding of Rome is shrouded in myth with tales of the twins Romulus and Remus suckled by a she-wolf. What is the traditional year given for its foundation?

4. Many of us learnt early in life that King Alfred burnt the cakes. He had the Danes on his mind. It was toward the end of which century?

5. Can you name the Chinese dynasty which began in the fourteenth century and ended in the eighteenth? This was an important period for China, both internally and through new contacts abroad.

6. From 1867 there has been an Emperor of Japan, but who ruled prior to this date from medieval times?

7. The generic name of plants is in Latin, and sometimes these words are long and difficult to recall. It can be useful for all languages to use the same terms, but what are the common popular names in English of the following flower and shrub or tree? myosotis; ilex

8. Brazil is the biggest South American country, and has the beautiful coastal town of Rio de Janeiro. It has the greatest mix of races anywhere. What is the official language?

9. Wellington, Auckland, Christchurch, three major towns of New Zealand. Can you say (1) which is the capital, (2) which is the largest town on North Island, (3) which is on South Island?

10. Australia, not forgetting the island of Tasmania, is fascinating in its long remoteness. Its land-mass makes up the smallest continent of the world. Can you complete the address by state or territory of the following towns, all near a coast? Brisbane, Darwin, Perth, Adelaide, Melbourne, Sydney

11. On 21 July 1969 the first man to do so stepped on the moon. What was his name?

12. The town we have known as Bucharest is the capital of which country?

13. There are three major religious groups for whom Jerusalem is a holy city. Can you name them?

14. Which is the longest river on our planet?

15. Mount Everest, or Sagarmatha, is the tallest mountain in the world. How many thousand feet does it pass?

Answers to Quick Quiz

		Score
1.	The Blue Whale	1
2.	Hinduism	1
3	753 BC	1
4.	The ninth century	1
5.	The Ming Dynasty	1
6.	The shogun warriors	1
7.	forget-me-not; holly	2
8.	Portuguese	1
9.	(1) Wellington, (2) Auckland, (3) Christchurch	3
10.	Queensland, Northern Territory, Western Australia, South Australia, Victoria, New South Wales	6
11.	Neil Armstrong	1
12.	Romania, sometimes as Rumania	1
13.	Christians, Jews, Muslems	3
14.	The Nile, Africa	1
15.	Over 29 thousand feet (over 8,800 metres)	1

Top Score   25

If you got some right – well done. You are on your way, or retaining well!

These varied and random questions have taken in the four corners of the earth as is euphemistically said, or in other words our spinning planet, plus moon, all maintained having powerful and essential gravity. Endless space remains difficult to conceive, our human conundrum.

Maximizing the Moment

Everybody has a place where he or she feels most at home. It is common for it to be the vicinity of birth but may be somewhere else. Perhaps when you were small you had a book illustrating the children of the world or you could have had some snap cards with, say, four pictures of Hawaiian girls in grass skirts and each having a lei, a hoopla garland of flowers at the neck.

However you began to be introduced to the variety of the world, for it still exists up to a point with diversity, you will be collecting additional information all your life. Finally, you may be visiting many different countries, so that friends or passing acquaintances will be showing you with pride their area's distinctive achievements and features. Hearing a new language, at any age, can be intriguing, even invigorating, and you may pick up at least a few fresh words along the way which can stay with you. We know our globe seems to get smaller as separated races mix and populations communicate more frequently, whether through electronics or other means. You never need feel as far distant as once people did. As is said, we are involved in all mankind.

If you are still growing, you want to take care to preserve the strength you now have. Then one day, hopefully, you will be able to realize your pipe-dreams. Schooling is not necessarily an easy time in this respect. It can throw an excessive amount of emphasis on the competitive element. Above all, you need to remember the sensitivity of the essential organ of the eye. Many of the discerning, including Darwin, have recognized this, and also the wonder of vision. It is therefore surprising how easily its importance gets overlooked.

Reading can tire the eyes, but if one consciously keeps one's whole frame relaxed while doing so, there should not be problems. Try not to get your head too close to the text, and it is always a good idea to look away into the distance occasionally. Do not forget that sight through the eye is connected to the brain, and rather than causing strain by peering unduly forward, one needs to realize that much of seeing is done far back in the head and also down in the neck. Breathe deeply, blink regularly, and if possible, for major work, have the light coming from behind or else the side.

Our lives are subject to change, as you know, and the scene, wherever you live, seems to be altering ever faster. Thus you are likely to find you need to absorb the printed word faster too. Quicker understanding is the order of any shift. Some people say you can just read down the centre of a page, but although one may be able to assess what a book is discussing, even solve a mystery story, it is not a proper way to obtain knowledge. Others claim you need just to concentrate on the long words, and there may be something in this attitude.

It is best to allow yourself adequate time. If you get called away, it is convenient to leave your bookmark over the page and reach the end of the first paragraph. Rather than the left-hand page, the verso, you can do something similar on the right-hand page, the recto, if that is the side you are reaching. You can stop again at the end of the first paragraph and leave the marker at the base of the page. Rushing can cause tension, which is to be avoided.

Computers can be short-cut aids, one has grasped no doubt, and, over time, methods have been spoken of to receive your night-time reading on the ceiling, with other fancied extensions, but the delight of reading an attractively produced book at your own pace, though paper gets used, is not likely ever to be completely replaced. These days, too, coloured illustrations are frequently introduced with great technical skill. Computerized e-books can be viewed as supplement, or alternative choice sometimes.

Taking a more general view of our conduct of life, has anybody at some stage said to you, 'be serene'? This is sound advice and achievable, when you think about it and then make the effort. It is not necessary, nor advisable, to rely on other people for your stability, which is much better coming naturally. Set your own goals. You may not have yet seen the painting by Brueghel, the Elder, a Flemish artist, of the blind leading the blind. The leader is taking the line down into a ditch. This could first strike you as very grim, but actually it can be seen as an allegory of what the world is about in fact. Nobody knows everything. You need to make up your own mind, perhaps with advice, concerning what you should do in any given situation.

`Never expect anything and you need never be disappointed' may be a bit extreme. It was a Japanese fellow who made the point that you want to face up to every predicament and not turn away. This will ensure, in the future, you will be able to overcome all eventualities. The Chinese can gain pleasure simply in sharing silence with each other. There is more to this world than man ever dreamed of, is a perception. Ends have new beginnings. Loss, or breakage, gives potential for fresh findings in keeping going forward. Muslems are comforted in error by the thought that only Allah is perfect.

These subjects can bring one on to the big issues, such as the aim of life, a vital consideration for peace of mind, which of course is primarily what is worth seeking. As Shakespeare quips in *Hamlet*, `to thine own self be true' and it will follow that you cannot 'then be false to any man'. It is clear that if you want to raise the quality of life, therefore, besides that of your personal affairs, you can start again with yourself, which is the easiest and best way.

The French philosopher, Pascal, was aware, as he states in his *Pensées,* that there is all to be gained, with regard to religion, in believing. Be ready to meet your maker. A well known American writer has proffered the opinion that all Americans and others too ultimately confess to and hope for an afterlife. 'All things are possible to those who believe' is an inspiration to many.

Our universe scientifically is not based on vague uncertainties. It revolves with accuracy and is mathematically precise. The moon, passing in front of the sun in a total eclipse to produce the shining corona in the darkness, is an incredible feat of multiple measurement from earth, if you ever have the opportunity to investigate the matter. Some, with eyes to see, consider it a miracle.

There are numerous religions which have developed over the centuries, embracing various truths and understanding about creation. The Bible has profound literary depths as well which can enter the psyche of a nation without full consciousness of it happening. The King James Authorized Version of 1611 has particular elegance, a resonance which is still valued today. It is in the fabric of the English-speaking background, and the discerning of all nationa-lities have appreciated it. This continues to be recognized at any rate by many older people The French also value in their language all the subtleties of the second person (case) singular - 'Tu', 'toi' and possessive 'ton' ... whereas we, the English, seem ready without much concern to drop 'Thou, thee, thine', in spite of, in religious matters, it containing clear reverence and respect. Not everyone will let the usage go.

Hymns, too, can instil a lasting hold on populations. One such is recently favoured *Amazing Grace* which has words by a Scot with music to accompany by a Swede, from the same country which produced the affecting dance responses to Abba and also widely revered *How Great Thou Art*. As we advance further in the twenty-first century, the world may appear to shrink, but it continues to change for all of us.

One thoughtful theme often expressed for advice is 'Do as you would be done by.' The Bible says, 'No man can serve two masters.' There is an existence to find which is beyond possessions, as you will discover if you have not done so already. Again, we are told, 'What shall it profit a man to gain the whole world and lose his own soul', and 'Perfect love casteth out fear.' We are all called to be children of God and therefore all important.

The most ancient honours dictum perpetuates *Honi soit qui mal y pense.* May none think ill, certainly no shame, through the words of this book, set down for enlightenment. It is worth pondering all these ideas and thereby setting a life on the right course. There is another saying which you could have had written in your autograph book. Quite possibly you did not, so I will end with this here: 'Life is as you make it.'

Acknowledgements

Sources Used

My thanks to:
The Hutchinson Encyclopedia, Encyclopedia Britannia; The Oxford Companions to American History, English Literature and Music; The People's Friend, BBC Wildlife Magazine; Oxford University Department of Zoology; *America 100 Years Ago* by Richard Lovett (1891); The American Airlines Information Service; *The Times, The Daily Telegraph, Radio Times;* and any other work which gave me a fact or notion.

Thank you, also, M.A. for last research details and D.E. for the typescript, thus enabling me to complete without delay. The latter named was my only MS reader!